THE 5-INGREDIENT VEGETARIAN COOKBOOK

The 5-Ingredient
Vegetarian
COOKBOOK

75 Effortless Recipes for Busy Cooks

Paige Rhodes

Photography by Laura Flippen

ROCKRIDGE
PRESS

For general information on our other products and services or to obtain technical support, please contact our Customer Care Department within the United States at (866) 744-2665, or outside the United States at (510) 253-0500.

Rockridge Press publishes its books in a variety of electronic and print formats. Some content that appears in print may not be available in electronic books, and vice versa.

TRADEMARKS: Rockridge Press and the Rockridge Press logo are trademarks or registered trademarks of Callisto Media Inc. and/or its affiliates, in the United States and other countries, and may not be used without written permission. All other trademarks are the property of their respective owners. Rockridge Press is not associated with any product or vendor mentioned in this book.

Interior and Cover Designer: Heather Krakora
Art Producer: Samantha Ulban
Editor: Anna Pulley
Production Editor: Matt Burnett
Production Manager: Riley Hoffman

Photography © 2021 Laura Flippen. Food styling by Laura Flippen.
Author photograph courtesy of Matt Johnson.

Cover: Chickpea Coconut Curry, page 62

ISBN: Print 978-1-64876-877-4
eBook 978-1-64876-743-2

R0

To my husband, Matt,
who willingly added
part-time vegetarian to his
already long list of
positive attributes
for the sake of research

Contents

Introduction

Hi there, I'm Paige Rhodes, and I am a cookbook author, food blogger, recipe developer, and lifelong meat eater. I know what you're thinking: *Why is someone who's not a full-time vegetarian writing a plant-based cookbook?* I'll tell you why. While I eat meat from time to time, I truly believe in the benefits of a vegetarian lifestyle. When I was professionally training in the culinary arts, it was ingrained in me that animal protein was an essential part of most meals. Today, we know that to be inherently false. Thankfully, the widespread popularity of plant-based eating has made its way into mainstream grocery stores, professional sports (many athletes are going vegan and vegetarian!), and beyond. I think it's vital to look at vegetarian recipes through the lens of a meat eater. After all, we want your meals to be just as nutritious and hearty as those centered on meat, and with this book, you can get it done with only 5 ingredients.

You may not even be a vegetarian yourself. Perhaps you're cooking for a mixed household of vegans, omnivores, pescatarians, and vegetarians all under one roof. You want to be able to please all of those people without even noticing the absence of meat. Maybe you have no intention of leaving your meat-eating ways behind, but you are looking to incorporate more fulfilling vegetarian days into your week, beyond meatless Mondays. Maybe you're a single parent who struggles to encourage your kids to eat their veggies, or perhaps food waste is a major issue for you, and you want to keep your ingredients as streamlined as possible. Whatever your intention is, welcome! This cookbook is for you.

Let's not pretend that there's any shortage of vegetable products available to plant eaters. Think about it. There are rows and rows of fresh and frozen vegetables, grains, and legumes stocking grocery store shelves. This could be one reason why a lot of home cooks are intimidated by cooking with plants. There are just too many options, and often, people don't know where to start. That's where the 5-ingredient recipes in this book come in. If you're one of these folks, I will steer you on the right path without overwhelming you. And we'll have fun doing it!

Let's talk about "meatless meats" for a minute. While there's now a plethora of faux meat products available on the market, this book will focus on whole-food cooking with the fewest ingredients possible. Of course, if you have a favorite soy crumble or tempeh bacon that you love, feel free to add it in wherever you like! Since there are only 5 ingredients (not counting salt, black pepper, oil, and water) in each recipe, there's plenty of room for you to adapt recipes according to what you have on hand. Recipes with minimal ingredients allow for more flexibility, improvisation, and creativity than other ingredient-packed dishes. I don't want you to feel limited by the 5-ingredient premise. Feel free to play with spices, add aromatics where you see fit, and, yes, even include meat, if desired. Experimentation is how favorite recipes are born!

My goal with this book is to start you on your journey to being a confident home cook. Whether you are dipping your toe in the vegetarian pool, trying to please your veggie-loving partner, or have been eating plant-based for years, I want you to have a solid base of fun and inventive recipes that you can cook for breakfast, lunch, dinner, dessert, snacks, and staples. I also want you to discover new, easy, and delicious meals that you'll come back to so many times the pages become oil stained and spattered with tomato. Cooking doesn't have to be cumbersome, and the chapters that follow will show you just how true that is.

CREAMY POLENTA
WITH ROASTED
BEETS, PAGE 73

CHAPTER ONE

Cooking Vegetarian with 5 Ingredients

Before we get to the drool-worthy recipes, I have a few points to go over. Maybe you picked up this book on a whim and you're wondering what the hullabaloo is about 5-ingredient cooking. In this chapter, I'm going to talk about the basics, what staples to keep in your arsenal, and why this method of cooking is perfect for vegetarianism. By the end, you should be more than convinced that delicious plant-centric meals are both attainable and ideal using the 5-ingredient method.

5-Ingredient Basics

As a former culinary school student and current food blogger, I've spent the better part of 10 years figuring out where my cooking strengths lie. I enjoy bringing delicious recipes into the homes of everyday cooks and showing them that nutritious and simple food is easily within their grasp. Being able to cook a full dish with only 5 ingredients may seem next to impossible, but it's more achievable than you'd imagine. If you have ever thought, *Do I really need to go buy a bay leaf for this soup?* the 5-ingredient method may already be something you've unintentionally set your sights on.

We're all busy these days. Whether you're a twentysomething cooking in your very first kitchen or an empty nester with a packed social calendar, there's something we would all rather be doing than sweating in the kitchen. To that end, 5-ingredient cooking hits the sweet spot. Using the best that vegetarian cooking has to offer, you can create stunning recipes that will produce limited waste and be easy on your wallet, all while pleasing your palate. Whether you're a freshly birthed veggie lover who needs a place to start or a seasoned pro who craves some new inspiration, everyone can benefit from the basics I'm about to share with you.

THE FOREVER STAPLES

The Forever Staples are the four ingredients that I recommend you keep in your kitchen at all times, and they're probably already there. They also don't count toward the 5 ingredients needed for the recipes in this book. While the temptation was there to add more than four to the list, I wanted to stay as true to the philosophy of the book as possible. The truth is, you can do a lot with some salt, black pepper, oil, and water. Think of these as your desert island must-haves.

1. **Salt** – So simple, yet so complex. It can be overwhelming to see dozens of salt options in the grocery store. My go-to for cooking is kosher salt; it's what I used when testing the recipes in this book. It has a coarse yet light texture and is less salty than table salt, which means it's more forgiving if you accidentally oversalt your food. If you wish to use a finishing salt, I'd recommend a flaky sea salt that will add a nice bite to the flavor of your food. But for cooking and the purposes of this book, it's kosher salt all the way.

2. **Freshly ground black pepper –** Just like coffee, when black pepper is freshly ground, it has a much fresher, more prominent flavor. I would recommend buying a refillable pepper grinder that you can fill with whole peppercorns as needed. You can purchase black peppercorns in bulk, and they keep for at least a year in a cool, dry space. The fine ground pepper that comes in a shaker at the store can be bitter and lose its flavor sitting on the shelf, so it's already started to deteriorate before you can even begin cooking with it.

3. **Oil –** Oils, like salts, can boggle the mind due to the sheer number of options on the grocery store shelves. Olive oil alone can include choices of virgin, extra-virgin, extra-light, cold-pressed, and refined. Beyond that, there are vegetable, canola, avocado, coconut, and peanut oils, and who knows what new oils may be in the works. Extra-virgin olive oil is what I've mostly cooked with for years with great results. That being said, if you have another neutral-flavored oil that you love and swear by, then by all means, use that.

4. **Water –** One of the ingredients I toyed with adding to this list was vegetable stock. From soups to pasta, vegetable stock is an ingredient that just rounds out a dish. Water does have a similar effect, though. As long as you're properly seasoning your food in other ways, adding water to a dish stretches out those flavors and gives every ingredient in the recipe room to groove. Just know that if you happen to have vegetable stock or broth in your pantry already, it makes a fine substitution for water in the savory recipes.

Vegetarian Cooking Made Simple

The truth is, sometimes we overdo it when attempting to go vegetarian or incorporate more plant-based meals into our meat-centric diets. "Less is more" is a common phrase for a good reason. While the recipes in this book contain only 5 ingredients, they are carefully chosen—each packing a major flavor punch, creating less waste, and meant to help you see how simple your meatless journey can be. Throughout this book, we'll be getting back to basics and simplifying the way you build vegetarian meals for yourself and your family, without sacrificing flavor.

HEARTY RECIPES

If you tend to feel a tiny gnaw in the pit of your stomach when you think about forgoing meat for the vegetarian option, hear this: You will be satisfied! In the chapters that follow, you'll find nourishing pasta dishes, filling plant-based salads, and robust breakfast recipes that will keep you satiated until your next meal. By combining certain ingredients like rice and beans to make a complete protein (meaning they contain all the essential amino acids), using grains like quinoa, and incorporating seeds and nuts, you can achieve carnivorous levels of fullness and satisfaction every step of the way. Centering your meals on plants doesn't have to make you feel like you're missing out. Comforting dishes like Eggplant Parmesan Roulades (page 65) and Creamy Butternut Squash Rigatoni (page 82) are wholesome and hearty and will make you feel like you're in the know, not missing out. In fact, serve any of the recipes in this book to a meat eater and be prepared to have them question everything they know.

EASY ADAPTATIONS

Even though all of the recipes in this cookbook are 5 ingredients or fewer (save for the aforementioned handful of pantry staples), I promise I won't stand guard in your kitchen to make sure you stick to that limit. I'm a firm believer that recipes should be fluid and rules have no place in the kitchen—beyond those that ensure safety, of course. If you feel that the pasta dish you're preparing would benefit from a splash of white wine, don't hold back. Would a drizzle of balsamic vinegar send that soup over the edge? Be my guest. Along with putting your own home chef spin on them, most of these recipes can easily be adapted to vegan, dairy-free, or gluten-free requirements if they aren't already, so keep your eyes peeled for substitution suggestions throughout the chapters, as well. Also check out Cooking for Everyone, page 6. Since the recipes are already minimal, the likelihood of having to substitute more than a couple of ingredients to fit your diet is low.

LESS WASTE

The fewer ingredients you use in a recipe, the less likely you are to create excess (and consequently, waste) in your kitchen. The short ingredient list *doesn't* equate to a lack of flavor. You'd be surprised what a dash of soy sauce, a drizzle of tahini, or a pinch of red pepper flakes can bring to a 5-ingredient dish. Streamlining your ingredients means that you will end up with recipes that are brimming with nuanced flavors that elevate instead of compete. This straightforward, utterly palatable experience will leave you wondering why you never simplified your cooking before.

You'll notice throughout this book that some ingredients are used repetitively but in different ways. If a recipe calls for coconut milk and you don't use the whole can, you can quickly find another recipe to make later in the week to finish it off, meaning less waste and more cost-effective meals.

QUICK PREP

Let's take the convenience factor of 5-ingredient meals up one more notch. Many of the ingredients in the chapters rely on basic spices and aromatics like onion and garlic to form the base of the recipe. If you don't feel like whipping out your cutting board, quick fixes like prechopped garlic and frozen veggies will be a huge time-saver for you. I also love picking up items like frozen brown rice and quinoa that can be easily thrown into recipes or microwaved as a nutrient-dense side. Even if you do take the time to prep what few ingredients there are yourself, it won't take you any more than 10 minutes, and honestly, it's a nice way to zone out for a few minutes and do something for yourself—pretend you're on a cooking show.

COOKING FOR EVERYONE

The great thing about this book is that there is something for everyone. More than ever, our households are a fusion of people with many different tastes, preferences, and restrictions. Whether you and your partner have made a pact to go meat free a couple of days a week or your newly strict vegetarian son suddenly needs three square veggie-based meals a day, I've got you covered.

Also, if you're an omnivore who's new to cooking for a vegetarian, know that I've been in the same situation. It's easy to avoid adding large pieces of meat when preparing a vegetarian meal, but as a meat eater, it's important to be mindful of small additions that you normally may not pay attention to. For example, you may not think about tossing some bacon bits into a salad or using fish sauce in your pad Thai. But since the recipes in this book contain only 5 ingredients, it's easy to follow the directions and avoid any pesky add-in accidents.

On the other hand, you may be a vegetarian who's cooking for the biggest beef lover, and you still want to please them without having to make two meals. Easy peasy. Does your girlfriend ask for steak every night? Try the Philly Cheese Portobello Subs (page 55) to satiate even the most carnivorous craving. Is breakfast a big deal in your house? Make a sweet and savory spread with the Farmers' Market Hash (page 26) and Coconut Chocolate Chia Pudding (page 16). The Creamy Coconut Vermicelli (page 90) is perfect for when you're dying to order takeout, and the Creamy Polenta with Roasted Beets (page 73) just screams date night. The approachable, fuss-free recipes in this book will show even the harshest of vegetarian naysayers that the plant-based way of life is more than "meats" the eye.

Setting Up Your Simple Veggie Kitchen

Beyond The Forever Staples (page 2), it's important to keep your pantry, refrigerator, and freezer stocked with essentials so you can bet on dinner success every night of the week. Since these recipes only require a handful of ingredients, the more you keep your kitchen fully equipped, the more you can pick and choose your meals throughout the week without having to worry about last-minute trips to the grocery store. To start, give your kitchen a good cleanout. Toss, compost, or recycle anything that's expired. Then, open your notes app or grab a pen or pencil and make a comprehensive list of anything you don't already have among the following ingredients.

ESSENTIALS TO STOCK

Aromatics – Garlic and onions are the main aromatics in so many recipes. I also like to have garlic powder and onion powder on hand at all times.

Balsamic vinegar – You can't have too many vinegar options in your kitchen. If I have to pick, my favorite is definitely balsamic for its sharp tang and subtle sweetness. It's used to make my Balsamic Glaze (page 105), used in many recipes.

Canned beans – Garbanzo beans and black beans are unparalleled in a vegetarian pantry. There's nothing like fresh Lemon Hummus (page 32) for an afternoon snack, and beans are great over salads or tucked into Quinoa Stuffed Peppers (page 63).

Canned tomatoes – I recommend keeping a variety of different canned tomatoes in your pantry. Crushed tomatoes, diced tomatoes, and tomato sauce are some great options to use in stews and pasta.

Cauliflower – Buy it by the whole head, and you can use it to make cauliflower rice, slice it into steaks, or break it into florets to use in many recipes. Keep some bags of frozen cauliflower on hand, too, for quick convenience in a pinch.

Chia seeds – These little seeds are packed with so many nutrients, like fiber and heart-healthy omega-3s, that vegetarians need in their diets; they're also a complete protein. Perfect for breakfast, snacks, or even a fun dessert, you'll want to try them in the Raspberry Chia Mousse (page 98).

Citrus – Citrus is an easy one-stop shop when it comes to adding a ton of bright flavor to a dish. We'll use both the zest and the juice of lemons and limes frequently in this book.

Eggs – Whether you're making one of the delicious breakfast recipes or rich Lava Cake (page 102), large eggs are a crucial part of vegetarian cooking that you must always keep stocked in your refrigerator.

Honey – Both sweet and savory dishes can easily get a leg up with a drizzle of honey. Quick tip: Whisk a quarter cup of honey with two teaspoons of hot sauce for a sensational pizza topping.

Maple syrup – For vegan cooking, pure maple syrup can usually be substituted for honey. Either way, it's a great natural sweetener to keep in the pantry.

Parmesan cheese – Parmesan will make every recipe seem like it was much more difficult to make. I recommend buying a whole wedge or grated Parmesan, which melts much more nicely than shredded.

Rice – Rice, along with lentils and quinoa, is perfect for adding bulk to bowls, soups, and salads. All of these can be purchased precooked in the freezer aisle and can be used interchangeably in most recipes.

Vegetable broth – Plant-based soups would be nothing without vegetable broth. Although you can usually swap it for water in a pinch, broth adds so much rich flavor to any one-pot meal and will really take any dish to the next level.

SHOPPING AND MEAL PREP

Between budgetary concerns, time restraints, and different tastes of household members, grocery shopping can be hard enough. Now, add the fact that you're just starting on your vegetarian journey or sharing a home (and refrigerator) with meat eaters, and things start to feel more complicated. Most grocery stores have apps or websites that allow you to order your groceries online to be picked up or delivered. I totally recommend taking advantage of this service while you're getting used to buying different foods that you might not be familiar with. Make a running list. And whenever you see a recipe that you like, write the ingredients down or go straight to the grocery store's app or website and add those ingredients to your cart. The same applies for the Essentials to Stock (page 7) and The Forever Staples (page 2). Go ahead and add those to your "favorites" (yes, store apps offer this feature!) and you never have to think about it again.

You may not want someone else choosing your produce. I get it! Go ahead and order your food for pickup, then get there a few minutes early and choose your own produce. Reusable mesh vegetable bags are great for when you go to the grocery to get your produce. Glass jars are also an economical choice so you can choose your own items like dried goods in bulk for the lowest price possible. Ultimately, having someone shop for you may seem like a luxury, but any service charge you pay for this will be offset by the fact that you'll avoid impulse purchases!

When it comes to prepping meals for the week, think about color-coding your containers: The meat eaters get red containers, the vegetarians get green ones, and so on. This way, there's no cross-contamination (or confusion) between the two. Since we're not dealing with animal products that have to be cooked to a certain temperature, you can undercook your meals slightly when meal prepping so when you reheat it, the dish doesn't become soggy or overcooked.

TOOLS AND EQUIPMENT

Almost as important as the ingredients are the tools used to cook the meal. If you fill your cabinets with a few fundamental utensils, gadgets, and pans, then there's nothing standing in your way. The following tools will make easy and efficient work of your meal prep.

As far as small tools go, **wooden spoons** will be the workhorse in your kitchen. A round one, a slotted one, and a straight-edged wooden spoon will be all you need to have in rotation.

A **metal whisk** and a **zester** for zesting citrus, grating Parmesan, or finely mincing garlic are two of my often used tools in the kitchen.

A **ladle** is a must for scooping all those soups you'll be making, and a **colander** is essential for draining pasta and canned beans. If you have a big family, I recommend a large colander for pasta and potatoes and a small one for draining and rinsing beans and berries.

You'll use a **blender** in recipes like the Quick Blender Salsa (page 31) and Tropical Smoothie Bowl (page 20). A blender is also very handy if you don't have a food processor.

A set of **stainless-steel mixing bowls** will be used in nearly every dish you make; they are a priceless addition to any kitchen collection.

Not a fan of cleanup? Try picking up a **silicone baking mat** for easy baking sheet cleanup that doesn't waste aluminum foil or parchment paper.

Of course, two of the most used tools in your kitchen that can't be replaced are a good **chef's knife** and **cutting board**. I would recommend an 8- or 10-inch knife with a full tang, which means the steel of the knife runs to the back of the handle. I mentioned earlier using a color-coding system with your food storage containers. I'd recommend opting for the same system when it comes to cutting boards, marking one for meat and another for veggies. While they can't be run through the dishwasher, I love the sustainability of wood and bamboo cutting boards. Try marking the bottoms with a colored permanent marker to differentiate them and avoid cross-contamination.

An 8- to 10-inch **nonstick skillet** is perfect for everything from scrambled eggs to quesadillas.

Investing in a few **glass jars with lids** will allow you to prep dishes like the Yogurt Panna Cotta (page 99) and store condiments and sauces like Honey Mustard Barbecue Sauce (page 103) and Simple Pesto (page 106).

ONE-POT WONDERS

On busy weeknights, there's nothing better than dirtying only one vessel in the process of cooking your 5-ingredient meal. One-pot dinners ensure that all the ingredients are done at the same time and tend to get on the table in a flash. Plus, cleanup is a breeze! My number-one tool to further simplify your cooking journey is a **cast-iron skillet**. A 10-inch will serve you well for most dishes, but fair warning, once you use one, you'll likely want it in different sizes.

Next up for one-pot wonders is a 5½-quart enameled **Dutch oven**. Whatever soup, stew, or pasta you're making will thrive in this multi-purpose pot that is used often in this book. Pro tip: Make sure you're scraping off all the yummy bits of food stuck to the bottom of the pot for extra flavor.

A **rimmed baking sheet** or **sheet pan** (or two) is a no-brainer. Pick up a set with a few different sizes and you can have cookies baking while you're roasting potatoes.

For all the casseroles and baked pasta dishes you'll want to make on cold nights, a **baking dish** is a necessary purchase. Opt for a glass dish for even and consistent heating and a set with both an 8-by-8-inch and a 13-by-9-inch for good measure.

About the Recipes

Whittling down a recipe to only 5 ingredients wasn't an easy task, but it's one that proved very rewarding. The truth is, we don't need a ton of fuss with our meals. Sure, it's fun to go all-out on a special occasion, but it's completely possible to create a mouthwatering plant-focused meal with minimal ingredients. Some of my favorite recipes lie within these pages. From a healthy riff on one of my grandpa's favorite store-bought cookies (Chocolate Rice Crunch Cookies, page 100) to the Cucumber Tea Sandwiches (page 50) that were inspired by a regional dish native to my home state of Kentucky, a piece of me is in each one. If you grew up in the '90s like me or have kids of your own, you'll love the After-School Noodle O's (page 92) and Fruity Cereal Bars (page 37) that bring a hint of nostalgia. Ultimately, the recipes in this book were made to be creative, fun, and well-rounded, both with regard to nutrition and flavor.

LABELS

Every recipe in this book is designed to help guide you, depending on what you're specifically looking for. At the top of each recipe, you'll find labels that indicate various dietary alerts as well as what recipe to pick based on your current time restrictions or needs.

> The **Vegan** label indicates recipes that are completely plant-based.
>
> The **Under 30 Minutes** label is for recipes that take a half hour or less to prep and cook from start to finish. (We can all use that on busy nights, right?)
>
> When you're looking for a recipe that's made entirely in one cooking vessel, you'll find the **One-Pot** label listed on recipes that apply.
>
> The **Freezer-Friendly** label is for recipes that freeze and reheat well for future meal planning. Unless stated otherwise, dishes labeled as such should last three months in an airtight container in the freezer.
>
> **Gluten-Free**, **Dairy-Free**, and **Nut-Free** labels appear where applicable.

TIPS

On many of the recipes that follow, you'll see a tip at the bottom that will provide helpful information for preparing the dish. A tip may refer to the cooking process, explain how to simplify the dish even further, help you with prepping the meal, or even speed your cleanup. A tip could also offer notes on picking perfect produce, where to search for an ingredient, or how to store a dish. If you need to substitute an ingredient, this is also the place where you would want to look. I may suggest a swap for a high-allergen ingredient or a polarizing flavor that some people may not love (looking at you, cilantro). The good news is, with only 5 ingredients per recipe, you likely won't have any trouble making your meal come together with ease.

KALE AND TOMATO
BREAKFAST PIZZA,
PAGE 27

CHAPTER TWO

Breakfast and Brunch

COCONUT CHOCOLATE CHIA PUDDING

DAIRY-FREE, GLUTEN-FREE, NUT-FREE, ONE-POT, VEGAN

Serves 4   **Prep time:** 5 minutes, plus 4 hours to chill

Pudding for breakfast? Yes, please! Chia seeds are one of the most nutrition-ally packed ingredients you can keep in your vegetarian pantry, and they're just right for prepping healthy and delicious breakfasts for the week. Full of fiber, omega-3 fatty acids, and high-quality protein, chia seeds are everything you could want for a plant-based meal. In this recipe, chia seeds are used to thicken the pudding and keep you full all morning long.

2 cups coconut milk

½ cup chia seeds

¼ cup cocoa powder

¼ cup maple syrup

¼ cup toasted coconut flakes

1. In a medium bowl, whisk together the coco-nut milk, chia seeds, cocoa powder, and maple syrup until well combined.

2. Pour the pudding into 4 individual glass jars, cover, and place in the refrigerator for at least 4 hours or overnight. Before serving, top with the toasted coconut flakes.

INGREDIENT TIP: Any milk would work great here. Almond milk, soy milk, and oat milk are all great substitutions, as is regular dairy milk if dairy is not a concern.

CINNAMON ORANGE GRANOLA

DAIRY-FREE, FREEZER-FRIENDLY, GLUTEN-FREE, NUT-FREE, ONE-POT

Makes 3 cups   **Prep time:** 10 minutes   **Cook time:** 30 minutes

Granola is the chameleon of the breakfast world. Whether you're pairing it with Greek yogurt, eating it as cereal, or using it as an ice cream topping, there's nothing that granola can't make better. A good basic recipe is a must in your arsenal, and this one is subtly spiced with cinnamon and orange zest to give you a great base. From there, you can add flaxseed, nuts, vanilla, chocolate chips—whatever your heart desires.

3 cups old-fashioned rolled oats (labeled gluten-free)

¼ cup brown sugar

½ teaspoon cinnamon

¼ teaspoon salt

1½ tablespoons olive oil

⅓ cup honey

2 tablespoons orange zest

1. Preheat the oven to 300°F. Line a baking sheet with a silicone mat or parchment paper.

2. In a large bowl, combine the oats, brown sugar, cinnamon, and salt and mix together.

3. In a small bowl, combine the olive oil, honey, and orange zest and stir. Pour the wet mixture over the oat mixture and stir until the oats are well coated.

4. Spread the mixture on the prepared baking sheet in an even layer.

5. Bake for about 30 minutes, or until the granola is golden brown and fragrant.

MAKE-AHEAD TIP: Homemade granola will last anywhere from two to four weeks in an airtight container. Check to make sure the granola is still crispy, and if it is, you're good to go. You can also freeze your granola in an airtight container for up to six months.

BANANA WALNUT OATMEAL

DAIRY-FREE, GLUTEN-FREE, ONE-POT, UNDER 30 MINUTES, VEGAN

Serves 4   **Prep time:** 5 minutes   **Cook time:** 10 minutes

There's nothing more comforting than a big bowl of oatmeal. Imagine your favorite slice of banana nut bread—that's the flavor you're getting with this oatmeal recipe. There's a reason why oats have been a go-to breakfast for families for so long. They're naturally gluten-free and contain more protein and fat than other grains. These perks, along with their high carbohydrate and fiber content, mean you'll stay satisfied into the afternoon.

4 ripe medium bananas, peeled

4 cups water, plus more if needed

2 cups old-fashioned rolled oats (see tip)

2 tablespoons maple syrup

1 teaspoon ground cinnamon

¼ teaspoon salt

¼ cup chopped walnuts

1. In a medium bowl, mash the bananas with a fork until creamy. Set aside.

2. In a medium saucepan over high heat, bring the water to a boil, then reduce the heat to a simmer. Stir in the oats and cook for about 4 minutes, stirring occasionally. Stir in the maple syrup, cinnamon, and salt.

3. Remove the pot from the heat and stir in the mashed bananas. If the oats are too thick, add a bit more water to thin them out. Portion the oatmeal into bowls and top them with the chopped walnuts. Serve warm.

INGREDIENT TIP: Oats are naturally gluten-free, but they are often cross-contaminated in transport. Check the label to make sure they're certified gluten-free if you have a sensitivity or allergy.

ZESTY PAPAYA MANGO SALAD

DAIRY-FREE, GLUTEN-FREE, NUT-FREE, ONE-POT, UNDER 30 MINUTES
Serves 4   **Prep time:** 10 minutes

If you're like me, you may find yourself getting bored with the standard meal prep you're used to. This fruit salad is perfect to prep at the start of the week and will make you feel like you're lying poolside! Plus, the cayenne will start your taste buds' morning off with a bang. This fun salad will have you coming back day after day for its refreshing goodness.

¼ cup honey

1 tablespoon freshly squeezed lime juice

1 tablespoon lime zest

¼ teaspoon cayenne pepper

Pinch salt

2 papayas, peeled, seeded, and diced

2 mangos, peeled, pitted, and diced

In a large bowl, whisk together the honey, lime juice, lime zest, cayenne pepper, and salt until smooth. Add the papaya and mango and toss well to fully coat. Chill until ready to serve.

INGREDIENT TIP: This recipe works great with so many tropical fruits. Try swapping the papaya or mango for a small, ripe pineapple, a few kiwis, watermelon, star fruit, or dragon fruit. Frozen fruit also works well, just allow it to thaw in the refrigerator before using it. To make this vegan, use maple syrup in place of the honey.

TROPICAL SMOOTHIE BOWL

DAIRY-FREE, GLUTEN-FREE, NUT-FREE, ONE-POT, UNDER 30 MINUTES, VEGAN

Serves 4   **Prep time:** 10 minutes

This tropical smoothie bowl is basically like having sorbet for breakfast, and I'm not one bit upset about it. Making the perfect smoothie bowl can take a bit of patience, since there's not as much liquid as in a regular smoothie, but it's so worth the extra bit of attention. I like topping mine with a shake of chili-lime seasoning and toasted coconut, a few big spoonfuls of Cinnamon Orange Granola (page 17) for crunch, or more sliced fruit.

2 cups coconut milk

2 cups frozen pineapple

2 large bananas, peeled and frozen

1 cup coconut yogurt

½ cup frozen mango

1. In the pitcher of a high-powered blender, combine the coconut milk, pineapple, bananas, yogurt, and mango. Blend until thoroughly combined and smooth. Stop the blender occasionally to scrape down the sides and move things around.

2. Scoop the smoothie into bowls and top with desired toppings.

VARIATION TIP: Trying to up your intake of leafy greens? Add in a couple handfuls of fresh spinach or kale for a nutritional boost. If you're serving kids, they'll probably love the bright green color and won't be able to taste the greens at all—just those delicious fruit flavors.

EGG WHITE QUESADILLA

FREEZER-FRIENDLY, NUT-FREE, ONE-POT, UNDER 30 MINUTES

Serves 4   **Prep time:** 10 minutes   **Cook time:** 10 minutes

Handheld breakfasts that you can eat on the go are in a league of their own. Bonus points if they can be prepped and frozen for a rainy (aka busy) day. This healthy, colorful, and filling quesadilla happens to be just that kind of meal, and the whole family will look forward to it before school or work.

6 large egg whites

½ teaspoon salt

¼ teaspoon freshly ground black pepper

1 tablespoon olive oil

1 red bell pepper, diced

4 (8-inch) flour tortillas

1 cup shredded Cheddar cheese

1 avocado, thinly sliced

1. In a medium bowl, whisk together the egg whites, salt, and black pepper.

2. Heat the oil in a large nonstick skillet over medium heat. Add the bell pepper and sauté for about 5 minutes, until the peppers begin to soften. Add the egg white mixture to the pan and cook, undisturbed, for 1 to 2 minutes, until the eggs begin to solidify. Using a rubber spatula, gently push the eggs to the center of the skillet for about 2 minutes, until just set. Immediately transfer the cooked eggs and bell peppers to a bowl.

3. Preheat the oven to 200°F or set it to "warm." Place an unlined baking sheet in the oven while it preheats.

4. Carefully wipe out the skillet with a paper towel and return it to the stove over medium-high heat. Lay 1 tortilla flat in the pan and sprinkle a quarter of the shredded Cheddar cheese on half of it. Top the cheese with a quarter of the scrambled egg whites and a quarter of the sliced avocado.

CONTINUED →

5. Cook for 1 to 2 minutes. When the tortilla turns just golden brown, fold it in half, pressing it with a spatula to flatten it.

6. Transfer the quesadilla to the prepared baking sheet in the oven to keep warm. Repeat with the remaining ingredients to make 3 more quesadillas.

MAKE-AHEAD TIP: To freeze, assemble the quesadillas without toasting the tortilla in the pan. Make sure the tortillas are at room temperature so they don't crack while folding them in half. Wrap each quesadilla individually in aluminum foil and freeze them in a single layer. Once frozen, transfer the quesadillas to a reusable freezer bag and freeze for up to two months. To cook frozen quesadillas, remove the foil and warm the quesadilla in the microwave for one to two minutes to thaw, then cook as directed in the skillet.

CRUSTLESS SPINACH AND GRUYÈRE QUICHE

FREEZER-FRIENDLY, GLUTEN-FREE, NUT-FREE, ONE-POT

Serves 4   **Prep time:** 10 minutes   **Cook time:** 35 minutes, plus 5 minutes to rest

No brunch spread is complete without quiche (and mimosas). This rich and hearty pie has a classic quiche base without the stress of dealing with pie crust. Add some nutrient-packed spinach and a big sprinkle of Gruyère cheese, and you're on your way to a dish that you'll serve over and over again—on weekends and beyond. Try serving this quiche with a lemon-dressed arugula salad or with simple roasted potatoes to complete the meal.

Olive oil or nonstick cooking spray, for greasing

4 large eggs

½ cup heavy (whipping) cream

½ cup whole milk

½ teaspoon salt

¼ teaspoon freshly ground black pepper

1 (10-ounce) package frozen spinach, thawed

1 cup shredded Gruyère cheese

1. Preheat the oven to 375°F and liberally grease a standard pie pan with olive oil or nonstick cooking spray.

2. In a medium bowl, whisk together the eggs, cream, milk, salt, and pepper. Pour the egg mixture into the prepared pie pan.

3. Using a clean kitchen towel or paper towels, squeeze out the excess moisture from the thawed spinach. Scatter the spinach and shredded cheese over the top of the egg mixture.

4. Bake for 30 to 35 minutes, or until the eggs are just set. Allow the quiche to rest for 5 to 10 minutes before serving.

CONTINUED →

MAKE-AHEAD TIP: You can freeze this quiche after you fill it, but before you bake it. Place the filled quiche on a plate and freeze until firm. Once frozen, wrap it with aluminum foil and put it into a freezer bag. Freeze for up to one month. You can bake from frozen, but allow an additional 20 minutes of cooking time.

VARIATION TIP: If you wish to add a store-bought pie crust, preheat the oven to 375°F. Arrange the crust in your pie pan, then line it with parchment paper. Fill the crust evenly with dried beans or pie weights and bake for 15 to 16 minutes, until the crust starts to brown. Remove the pie crust from the oven and carefully lift the parchment paper with the beans or weights out of the pie crust. Prick the bottom crust with a fork. Return the pie crust to the oven for 7 to 8 minutes. Fill the crust as directed and bake for another 30 to 35 minutes.

BAKED EGGS IN TOMATOES WITH FETA

GLUTEN-FREE, NUT-FREE, ONE-POT, UNDER 30 MINUTES

Serves 4   **Prep time:** 5 minutes   **Cook time:** 20 minutes

From Middle Eastern *shakshuka* to Italian eggs in purgatory, baked eggs in tomatoes are a delicious meal enjoyed across the globe. This pared back version is perfect for serving to the whole family and can easily be spiced up with some red pepper flakes or smoked paprika. Try adding cooked lentils or drained canned chickpeas to bulk this up for dinner. Now, grab a crusty baguette and get scooping!

1 tablespoon olive oil

1 medium yellow onion, diced

1 (28-ounce) can crushed tomatoes

½ teaspoon dried oregano

¾ teaspoon salt, plus more as needed

¼ teaspoon freshly ground black pepper, plus more as needed

4 large eggs

4 ounces feta cheese, crumbled

1. Preheat the oven to 375°F.

2. Heat the oil in a large oven-safe pan over medium-high heat. Add the onion and sauté for about 3 minutes, until translucent. Stir in the tomatoes, oregano, salt, and pepper. Bring to a simmer and cook, stirring occasionally, for about 3 minutes, until slightly thickened.

3. Make four evenly spaced wells in the tomato sauce and break 1 egg into each well. Sprinkle the eggs with a pinch of additional salt and pepper. Transfer to the oven and bake for 9 to 12 minutes, until the whites are set but the yolks are still runny. Top with the crumbled feta cheese while warm and serve immediately.

FARMERS' MARKET HASH

DAIRY-FREE, GLUTEN-FREE, NUT-FREE, ONE-POT

Serves 4   **Prep time:** 10 minutes   **Cook time:** 25 minutes

Whenever I go out for brunch, I almost always order some form of hash as my main dish to go alongside my pancakes. Anyone else need to have something sweet and savory? Hash contains everything you need for a well-rounded meal: hearty potatoes, flavorful onions and bell peppers, kale for added nutrients, and eggs for a boost of protein. All you may need is a few dashes of hot sauce on top and you're good to go.

1½ tablespoons
olive oil

1 pound Yukon Gold
potatoes, diced small

1 small yellow
onion, diced

½ red bell
pepper, diced

2 cups kale, stems
removed and
roughly chopped

½ teaspoon salt, plus
more as needed

½ teaspoon freshly
ground black pepper,
plus more as needed

4 large eggs

1. Preheat the oven to 400°F.

2. Heat the oil in a medium cast-iron skillet over medium-high heat. Add the potatoes, onion, and bell pepper and cook for 7 to 8 minutes, stirring frequently, until the potatoes start to become tender. Add the kale, salt, and black pepper. Cook for 1 to 2 minutes, until the kale begins to wilt.

3. Make four evenly spaced wells in the hash mixture and break 1 egg into each well. Sprinkle the eggs with a pinch of additional salt and pepper. Transfer to the oven and bake for 9 to 12 minutes, until the egg whites are set but the yolks are still runny and the potatoes are fork-tender.

KALE AND TOMATO BREAKFAST PIZZA

NUT-FREE, ONE-POT, UNDER 30 MINUTES

Serves 4   **Prep time:** 10 minutes   **Cook time:** 20 minutes

Just a few things make me excited about getting out of bed in the morning, and pizza for breakfast is one of them. Store-bought pizza dough is a super handy grocery item to keep in the freezer for easy breakfasts, lunches, and dinners. Just pull the dough out of the freezer and pop it into the refrigerator the night before so it has time to thaw. Then, pile it with whatever toppings you've got on hand, bake, and enjoy!

1 (8-ounce) package pizza dough

1 tablespoon olive oil, plus more for oiling the pan

2 cups fresh kale, stems removed

2 cups shredded white Cheddar cheese

4 large eggs

3 Roma tomatoes, thinly sliced

½ teaspoon salt

¼ teaspoon freshly ground black pepper

1. Preheat the oven to 400°F. Roll or press the pizza dough onto an oiled baking sheet. Drizzle the olive oil onto the crust and brush it evenly over the surface. Arrange the kale evenly over the top, leaving about an inch bare around the edges. Evenly sprinkle the Cheddar over the kale. Make four evenly spaced wells between the kale and cheese, and crack 1 egg into each well.

2. Arrange the tomatoes around the eggs. Season the top of the eggs and tomatoes with the salt and pepper. Bake for 14 to 18 minutes, until the crust is crispy and the cheese is melted. Serve immediately.

CINNAMON APPLE CHIPS, PAGE 30

CHAPTER THREE

Snacks and Bites

CINNAMON APPLE CHIPS

DAIRY-FREE, GLUTEN-FREE, NUT-FREE, ONE-POT

Serves 4 **Prep time:** 10 minutes **Cook time:** 3½ hours

I distinctly remember the first time I ate a store-bought apple chip as a kid. It took me the whole bag to decide if I liked them or not—spoiler alert: I did. As an adult, these are still a go-to snack, and I love that they can easily be packed in a lunch box for noshing on busy days. They're great with pink or red apples like Honeycrisp, but if you love Granny Smiths, go for it.

3 large red apples

¾ teaspoon ground cinnamon

¼ teaspoon granulated sugar

1. Preheat the oven to 200°F. Line 2 baking sheets with silicone mats or parchment paper, and arrange the oven racks on the upper and lower third sections of the oven.

2. With a sharp knife or mandoline, slice the apples horizontally into ⅛-inch-thick rounds, discarding the apple seeds.

3. In a small bowl, toss together the cinnamon and sugar.

4. Arrange the apples in a single layer on the prepared baking sheets. Sprinkle them with the cinnamon-sugar mixture. Bake for 2½ hours, rotating the baking sheets halfway through. Turn off the oven and let the apples sit in the closed oven for 1 hour to continue to crisp and dehydrate.

VARIATION TIP: Warming spices like nutmeg, cloves, cardamom, and allspice are perfect for seasoning these apple chips. If using one of these, reduce the amount to ½ teaspoon as they pack more of a punch. You can even leave them plain if you wish, or use brown sugar in place of granulated sugar.

QUICK BLENDER SALSA

DAIRY-FREE, GLUTEN-FREE, NUT-FREE, ONE-POT, UNDER 30 MINUTES, VEGAN

Makes 3 cups   **Prep time:** 10 minutes

Raise your hand if the number-one reason you go to a Mexican restaurant is for the chips and salsa, followed by the margaritas, then the tacos. This restaurant-style salsa is mild, yet flavorful enough to please all palates. Thanks to the canned tomatoes, you don't have to wait for tomato season to roll around to make it, either.

1 (14.5-ounce) can fire-roasted diced tomatoes

1 (10-ounce) can diced tomatoes and green chiles, drained

½ medium white onion, diced

½ cup fresh cilantro

1 garlic clove, minced

¼ teaspoon salt

¼ teaspoon freshly ground black pepper

1. In the pitcher of a blender, combine the fire-roasted diced tomatoes and diced tomatoes and green chiles, the onion, cilantro, garlic, salt, and pepper. Pulse several times until everything is uniform and the consistency is to your liking. The onion pieces should be barely visible.

2. Taste and adjust the seasoning as necessary. The salsa will last for 7 to 10 days in an airtight container in the refrigerator.

VARIATION TIP: If you like things spicy, feel free to add a chopped jalapeño to the blender, as well. I also highly recommend a squeeze of lime juice to finish things off, if you have it on hand.

LEMON HUMMUS

DAIRY-FREE, GLUTEN-FREE, NUT-FREE, ONE-POT, UNDER 30 MINUTES, VEGAN
Makes 2 cups   **Prep time:** 10 minutes

Hummus is one of those dishes worth keeping around at all times. The whole family loves it, and it's so easy to make yourself. Plus, you can customize it however you like (see tip)! I will often scoop out some separately and add a spoonful of chili paste on top because I like mine spicy. This hummus, paired with some crudités or pita chips, will set you up for protein-packed snack success all week long.

1 (15-ounce) can chickpeas, drained and rinsed

2 garlic cloves, minced

Juice and zest of 1 lemon

2 tablespoons tahini

2 tablespoons olive oil, plus more for drizzling

½ teaspoon salt

½ teaspoon paprika

1. In a food processor or blender, combine the chickpeas, garlic, lemon juice and zest, tahini, oil, and salt. Blend until creamy, scraping down the sides as necessary.

2. Transfer the hummus to a bowl and sprinkle it with the paprika and an additional drizzle of oil. Serve. This hummus will keep in an airtight container in the refrigerator for 3 to 5 days.

VARIATION TIP: Just like the hummus you'd find at the grocery store, this homemade version lends itself to so many tasty toppings. Try adding a spoonful of chopped olives or roasted red peppers to the top, or a drizzle of Sriracha or Balsamic Glaze (page 105).

THREE-SEED CRACKERS

DAIRY-FREE, GLUTEN-FREE, NUT-FREE, VEGAN

Makes about 40 crackers   **Prep time:** 20 minutes   **Cook time:** 3 hours

No charcuterie or snack board is complete without an impressive homemade cracker. Whether you're spreading these crackers with almond butter, dipping them in Lemon Hummus (page 32), or eating them with sliced cheese, these multi-purpose crackers are more than worth the time and effort. Once the crackers are cooled, you can store them at room temperature in an airtight container for up to two weeks.

½ cup pumpkin seeds

1 cup flax meal

½ cup chia seeds

1 teaspoon salt

½ teaspoon garlic powder

½ teaspoon onion powder

1¼ cups water

1. Preheat the oven to 200°F.

2. Place the pumpkin seeds in a food processor and pulse several times, until it resembles flour.

3. In a large bowl, add the ground pumpkin meal, flax meal, chia seeds, salt, garlic powder, and onion powder. Add the water and stir until the mixture becomes a dough.

4. Divide the mixture in half and place the dough on two separate sheets of parchment paper. Place another piece of parchment paper on top of the dough and roll each to about ⅛-inch thick. Remove the top parchment and use a knife to score the mixture into evenly sized squares.

5. Place the parchment sheets with the perforated cracker dough onto two baking sheets and cook for 2½ to 3 hours, rotating the pans halfway through. The crackers should be dry to the touch when done. Allow the crackers to cool completely, then break them apart.

MARINATED CARROTS AND CAULIFLOWER

DAIRY-FREE, GLUTEN-FREE, NUT-FREE, ONE-POT, VEGAN

Makes 1 quart   **Prep time:** 10 minutes
Cook time: 20 minutes, plus 2 hours to chill

You can pickle or marinate just about anything, which I'm totally on board for. If you're tired of the same crudités you've been eating to get your veggies in, you're going to love this fun, simplified twist on Italian *giardiniera*. Eat it straight from the jar for a snack, or use it to top your subs, tacos, or even meatless hot dogs. For easy access, store it in a quart-size glass jar for up to two weeks.

1 tablespoon olive oil

1 cup freshly chopped cauliflower florets

2 medium carrots, peeled and sliced

2 garlic cloves, minced

1 tablespoon salt

1 teaspoon oregano

1 teaspoon freshly ground black pepper

1 cup water

1 cup white vinegar

1. Heat the oil in a large pan over medium heat. Add the cauliflower and carrot slices and sauté, stirring occasionally, for 5 minutes. Add the garlic, salt, oregano, and pepper. Stir and cook for about 1 minute more, until the garlic is fragrant.

2. Add the water and vinegar and bring to a boil. Reduce the heat to low and simmer for 10 minutes. Remove the pan from the heat and let cool to room temperature.

3. Transfer the vegetables and liquid to a jar to chill it in the refrigerator for at least 2 hours before serving.

BAKED PICKLE CHIPS

DAIRY-FREE, FREEZER-FRIENDLY, NUT-FREE, ONE-POT, UNDER 30 MINUTES

Serves 4   **Prep time:** 10 minutes   **Cook time:** 15 minutes

Name a better appetizer than fried pickles. I'll wait. This healthier version is still just as crispy and delicious without having to worry about oil splatter. These baked pickle chips are amazing served with Greek Yogurt Cucumber Ranch (page 104) or Garlic Aioli (page 107) for dipping. Have leftovers? One of my favorite tricks is adding them to salads for a tangy, crunchy bite.

2 tablespoons
all-purpose flour

½ teaspoon
smoked paprika

½ teaspoon freshly
ground black pepper

1 egg, lightly beaten

½ cup whole-wheat
panko bread crumbs

32 dill pickle slices

1. Preheat the oven to 400°F.

2. In a medium bowl, combine the flour, paprika, and pepper. Put the beaten egg in a small bowl and the panko crumbs in another medium bowl.

3. Pat the pickle slices dry on both sides. Dredge the pickles in the flour mixture, then the beaten egg, and finally, in the panko crumbs.

4. Arrange the pickles in a single layer on a baking sheet. Bake for about 8 minutes on each side, until crispy. Serve immediately.

   MAKE-AHEAD TIP: To freeze these pickles for later, proceed as directed through step 3. Place the breaded pickles in a single layer on a parchment-lined baking sheet or plates and freeze them for 20 minutes. Transfer the pickles to a freezer bag and store them in the freezer for up to two months. When you're ready to cook, you may need to add one minute of additional cook time to each side.

CRISPY CHIPOTLE CHICKPEAS

DAIRY-FREE, GLUTEN-FREE, NUT-FREE, ONE-POT, UNDER 30 MINUTES, VEGAN
Makes 2 cups   **Prep time:** 5 minutes   **Cook time:** 25 minutes

When I meal prep, I like to prepare elements that I can use throughout the week in different recipes, as well as for snacking. Precut veggies, hard-boiled eggs, and these crispy chipotle chickpeas are a few of my favorites to keep on hand. These chickpeas are an amazing crunchy chip alternative, and to boot, they're perfect in salads, on top of soups, and even tossed into pasta.

1 (15-ounce) can chickpeas, drained and rinsed

1 tablespoon olive oil

¼ teaspoon salt

¼ teaspoon freshly ground black pepper

¼ teaspoon chipotle chili powder

1. Preheat the oven to 450°F. Place an unlined baking sheet in the oven while it preheats.

2. Using a clean kitchen towel or paper towels, pat the chickpeas dry to eliminate excess moisture that would prevent crisping.

3. In a bowl, toss the dry chickpeas with the oil, salt, pepper, and chili powder.

4. Carefully remove the baking sheet from the oven. Pour the chickpeas onto the preheated baking sheet, give the pan a shake, and return it to the oven. Roast for 20 to 25 minutes, shaking the pan halfway through, until crispy.

FRUITY CEREAL BARS

NUT-FREE

Makes 20 bars   **Prep time:** 10 minutes
Cook time: 10 minutes, plus 20 minutes to chill

Before you go thinking that these bars are for kids only, keep in mind that you'll be hiding them from the children before long. Fruity cereal is my personal favorite to use, but you can experiment with any cereal you like. I think some of the best combinations are chocolate cereal dipped in chocolate, toasted cinnamon cereal dipped in white chocolate, and peanut butter cereal dipped in peanut butter chips. Hubba-hubba.

Nonstick
cooking spray

5 tablespoons
unsalted butter

7 cups mini
marshmallows

½ teaspoon salt

1 teaspoon
vanilla extract

6 cups fruity
O-shaped cereal

1 cup Greek
yogurt chips

1. Line an 8-by-8-inch sheet pan with parchment paper so the paper comes up both sides, and coat it with nonstick spray. Set aside.

2. In a large saucepan over low heat, melt the butter. Add the marshmallows and stir continuously until melted. Remove the saucepan from the heat and stir in the salt and vanilla. Pour the cereal into the melted marshmallow mixture and stir to coat.

3. Press the mixture into the prepared sheet pan. Place the pan in the refrigerator for 20 minutes.

4. Meanwhile, melt the Greek yogurt chips in a medium microwave-safe bowl in 30-second increments, stirring in between, until melted.

CONTINUED →

5. Remove the pan from the refrigerator and use the parchment paper to lift the hardened mixture out of the pan. Cut the mixture into bars and dip the bottom of each bar into the melted Greek yogurt chips, then set it on parchment paper. Once all the bars are dipped, drizzle more of the melted chips on top, if desired. Store in an airtight container in the refrigerator for up to 5 days.

INGREDIENT TIP: Greek yogurt chips are found with the chocolate chips in the grocery store. If you can't find them, white chocolate chips work just fine.

CHOCOLATE COCONUT ENERGY BALLS

DAIRY-FREE, FREEZER-FRIENDLY, GLUTEN-FREE, ONE-POT

Makes 16 energy balls   **Prep time:** 10 minutes, plus 1 hour to chill

If there's one thing we could all use more of, it's energy. These tasty little energy balls stave off hunger, thanks to the healthy fats, protein, and fiber in the peanut butter. They also provide sustained energy from the rolled oats that are slowly absorbed by your body. Pop a few in a container that you can throw in your purse or backpack, and they'll be more than enough to hold you over until your next meal.

1 cup old-fashioned rolled oats (labeled gluten-free)

½ cup peanut butter

¼ cup honey

¼ cup unsweetened shredded coconut

¼ cup mini semisweet chocolate chips

Pinch salt

1. In a large bowl, combine the oats, peanut butter, honey, coconut, chocolate chips, and salt and stir together well. Cover and refrigerate for 1 hour to chill and firm.

2. When chilled, roll the mixture into 1-inch balls. Store them in an airtight container in the refrigerator for up to 2 weeks.

MAKE-AHEAD TIP: These energy balls freeze and thaw well. Simply store them in an airtight container in the freezer for up to three months.

ALMOND BUTTER DATE BITES

DAIRY-FREE, FREEZER-FRIENDLY, GLUTEN-FREE, ONE-POT, UNDER 30 MINUTES, VEGAN

Makes 14 bites   **Prep time:** 15 minutes

Also known as bliss balls, date bites are a nutritional powerhouse. They're loaded with healthy fats, thanks to the nuts, and naturally sweetened with Medjool dates. You can buy dates anywhere these days, and they're a great way to appease that pesky sweet tooth. If you've had yours for a while and they look a bit dry, you can soak them in hot water for a few minutes before blending to reconstitute them. P.S. Don't forget to pit your dates (or buy them already pitted).

1 cup raw walnuts

½ cup raw cashews

10 Medjool dates, pitted

⅓ cup almond butter

1 teaspoon vanilla extract

¼ teaspoon salt

1 to 2 tablespoons water

1. In a food processor, combine the walnuts, cashews, dates, almond butter, vanilla, and salt. Process the ingredients until a smooth dough forms and there are no chunks of dates left. If needed, scrape the sides of the food processor a few times. If your dough looks too dry and isn't coming together, add 1 to 2 tablespoons of water and continue to process.

2. Once the mixture is evenly blended, roll the dough into 1-inch balls. Serve or store (see tip).

MAKE-AHEAD TIP: You can store these date bites at room temperature or chilled, depending on your preference. In the refrigerator, they remain firm and easy to transport for up to ten days. At room temperature, they're a bit softer and fudge-like, lasting three days. You can also freeze them in an airtight container for up to one month.

VEGETABLE SPRING
ROLLS, PAGE 49

CHAPTER FOUR

Soups, Sandwiches, and Salads

BOK CHOY RAMEN

DAIRY-FREE, FREEZER-FRIENDLY, NUT-FREE, ONE-POT, UNDER 30 MINUTES

Serves 4   **Prep time:** 5 minutes   **Cook time:** 20 minutes

With ramen, there are so many ways you can add flavor if you have the ingredients available. The five ingredients below are a great base and taste delicious as is, but feel free to add in minced garlic or ginger, shiitake mushrooms, miso paste, or red pepper flakes if you like. You can also add additional toppings like sliced scallions, Sriracha, julienned carrots, or sesame oil to your finished bowl.

4 cups
vegetable broth

2 tablespoons soy
sauce, plus more
for serving

2 heads baby bok
choy, thinly sliced

3 packages ramen
noodles, seasoning
packets discarded

4 soft-boiled eggs,
halved (see tip)

1. In a large pot or Dutch oven over medium-high heat, combine the vegetable broth and soy sauce and bring it to a boil. Reduce the heat and simmer.

2. Add the bok choy to the broth and simmer for 7 to 10 minutes, or until the greens are wilted. Add in the ramen noodles and simmer for about 3 minutes, until the noodles are tender.

3. Ladle the ramen and broth into serving bowls and top each with 2 soft-boiled egg halves and additional soy sauce, if desired.

COOKING TIP: To soft-boil your eggs, bring a medium pot of water to a boil. Carefully drop in the eggs and set a timer for six minutes. Have an ice bath ready and as soon as the time is up, transfer the eggs to the ice bath. Wait just until the eggs are cool enough to handle easily, then peel, halve, and serve.

GREEK LEMON ORZO SOUP

DAIRY-FREE, FREEZER-FRIENDLY, NUT-FREE, ONE-POT

Serves 4   **Prep time:** 10 minutes   **Cook time:** 30 minutes

This comforting lemon orzo soup is a simplified, vegetarian take on Greek avgolemono or "egg-lemon." The combination of eggs, lemon juice, and broth, heated until thickened, is a common way of thickening soups and sauces around the Mediterranean. Lucky for us, the result is a creamy soup with a pop of lemon flavor. Rice is more traditional if you wish to swap, but I love the texture that orzo adds to this dish.

**6 cups
vegetable broth**

½ teaspoon salt

**⅛ teaspoon freshly
ground black pepper**

1 cup uncooked orzo

**⅓ cup freshly
squeezed lemon juice**

2 large eggs

**¼ cup freshly
chopped dill**

1. In a large pot or Dutch oven, over medium-high heat, bring the vegetable broth to a boil. Season with the salt and pepper, and add the orzo. Cover the soup with the lid slightly askew, reduce the heat to low, and simmer for 15 minutes, stirring occasionally.

2. In a medium bowl, whisk together the lemon juice and eggs for about 2 minutes, until light and frothy.

3. Remove the soup from the heat and slowly whisk 2 cups of the hot soup into the egg mixture to temper the eggs. Slowly pour the egg mixture back into the pot, stirring constantly. Stir in the dill. Serve hot.

MAKE-AHEAD TIP: You can store this soup in an airtight container in the refrigerator for up to three days. You can also freeze it flat in freezer bags for up to six months. To reheat, thaw the soup in the refrigerator overnight, then reheat it on the stovetop over medium heat. You'll likely need a splash of water or vegetable broth to thin it out a bit.

TUSCAN WHITE BEAN SOUP

DAIRY-FREE, FREEZER-FRIENDLY, GLUTEN-FREE, NUT-FREE,
ONE-POT, UNDER 30 MINUTES, VEGAN

Serves 6   **Prep time:** 5 minutes   **Cook time:** 15 minutes

One of my favorite items to keep in my pantry to add flavor to recipes is sun-dried tomatoes in oil. You can use the olive oil that they're packed in to sauté with, and the tomatoes themselves explode with flavor. Most are seasoned with Italian herbs like oregano, basil, and parsley, so you're getting those wonderful flavors in your dish, as well. Grab a baguette because you'll want to sop up every bit of this soup.

2 tablespoons olive oil

4 garlic cloves, minced

2 tablespoons sun-dried tomatoes in oil, chopped

6 cups vegetable broth

1 teaspoon salt

½ teaspoon freshly ground black pepper

2 (15.5-ounce) cans great northern beans, drained and rinsed

2 cups baby kale

1. Heat the oil in a large pot or Dutch oven over medium heat. Stir in the garlic and sun-dried tomatoes and cook for about 1 minute, until fragrant. Add the vegetable broth, salt, and pepper. Bring the soup to a simmer and cook for 5 minutes.

2. Stir in the beans and continue to cook for another 5 minutes. Add the kale and allow it to wilt for 1 minute before serving.

TORTELLINI TOMATO SOUP

FREEZER-FRIENDLY, NUT-FREE, ONE-POT

Serves 6   **Prep time:** 10 minutes   **Cook time:** 1 hour

If you've never made homemade tomato soup, you've been missing out on a luscious and creamy comfort food that is so easy to whip up. To make it a bit more substantial, I added cheese tortellini because everything's better with pasta, but you're welcome to use spinach tortellini or whatever variety you have on hand. On a chilly day, you'd be hard-pressed to find something better than this soup with an Apple Cheddar Grilled Cheese (page 51).

3 tablespoons olive oil

½ yellow onion, diced

2 garlic cloves, minced

4 cups water

2 (28-ounce) cans crushed tomatoes with basil

1 teaspoon salt

½ teaspoon freshly ground black pepper

¾ cup heavy (whipping) cream

1 (20-ounce) bag cheese tortellini

1. Heat the oil in a large pot or Dutch oven over medium heat. Add the onion and sauté, stirring occasionally, for about 5 minutes, until softened. Stir in the garlic and cook for 1 minute more.

2. Pour in the water, then add the crushed tomatoes, salt, and pepper. Bring to a simmer and cook, stirring occasionally, for 30 minutes. Remove the soup from the heat and allow it to cool slightly.

3. Using a food processor or blender, carefully puree the soup until completely smooth. You may need to do this in batches. (Alternatively, you can use an immersion blender.) Return the soup to the pot, add the cream, and simmer over low heat for about 10 minutes, or until slightly thickened. Add the tortellini and simmer for 5 to 8 minutes, until the tortellini is cooked through. Serve warm.

BLACK BEAN CHILI

DAIRY-FREE, FREEZER-FRIENDLY, GLUTEN-FREE, NUT-FREE, ONE-POT, VEGAN

Serves 6   **Prep time:** 10 minutes   **Cook time:** 35 minutes

From their role in vegan burgers to soups and stews, black beans are a nutritional workhorse in the vegetarian kitchen. They're high in carbohydrates to keep you full, but they don't give you a pesky blood sugar spike. Black beans also provide sustained energy and optimize heart health to promote longevity. I love using them in chili recipes, where they can stand up to the Southwest flavors and shine.

2 tablespoons
olive oil

1 small yellow
onion, diced

2 tablespoons taco
seasoning

½ teaspoon salt

¼ teaspoon freshly
ground black pepper

2 (14.5-ounce)
cans fire-roasted
diced tomatoes and
green chiles

3 (14.5-ounce) cans
black beans, drained
and rinsed

1 cup frozen corn

1 cup water

1. Heat the oil in a large pot or Dutch oven over medium heat. Add the onion and sauté for 3 to 4 minutes. Add the taco seasoning, salt, and pepper and cook, stirring, for about 1 minute, until fragrant.

2. Add the diced tomatoes and green chiles, black beans, frozen corn, and water. Stir to combine. Reduce the heat to a simmer and cook, stirring occasionally, for 25 to 30 minutes. Serve warm.

SERVING TIP: This chili is fun to serve if you're watching the big game! Set up a toppings bar with bowls full of shredded Cheddar cheese, sour cream, avocado, cilantro, chives, tortilla strips, and plenty of hot sauce so everyone can top their chili as they wish.

VEGETABLE SPRING ROLLS

DAIRY-FREE, GLUTEN-FREE, NUT-FREE, ONE-POT, UNDER 30 MINUTES, VEGAN

Serves 4 **Prep time:** 20 minutes

Spring rolls are such a fun way to turn an everyday salad into something hand-held. If sweet chili sauce isn't your first choice for a dipping sauce, try whisking together a half cup of peanut butter with a half cup of water, two tablespoons of rice vinegar, two tablespoons of soy sauce, one tablespoon of maple syrup, and one teaspoon of sesame oil for an epic peanut sauce that you'll want to slather on just about everything.

12 rice paper wrappers

1 bunch fresh cilantro

2 carrots, peeled and julienned

1 English cucumber, thinly sliced

Sweet chili sauce, for dipping

1. Fill a shallow bowl with warm water and lightly moisten the surface of a cutting board. Dip a rice paper wrapper into the bowl of water, making sure the entire surface is moistened. Carefully transfer the damp rice paper wrapper onto the cutting board to fill.

2. Arrange some of the cilantro, carrots, and cucumber in rows in the middle of the rice paper, about 1 inch away from the edges of the wrapper.

3. Starting from the bottom, roll everything toward the middle. Fold the sides of the wrapper toward the center, and finish rolling up the spring roll. Repeat with the remaining rice paper and vegetables. Serve with sweet chili sauce for dipping.

CUCUMBER TEA SANDWICHES

NUT-FREE, UNDER 30 MINUTES

Serves 4   **Prep time:** 20 minutes

You'll feel like royalty when you're eating these delicate and delicious tea sandwiches. Fancy making a whole afternoon tea experience out of it? Build a spread consisting of English breakfast tea with honey, lemon, and cream for serving, along with light shortbread cookies and scones. I think even the queen herself would approve of this recipe that could be served to guests or taken to work for lunch.

2 large cucumbers,
1 peeled and seeded,
1 peeled and thinly
sliced, divided

2 scallions, white
and green parts,
roughly chopped

2 (8-ounce) packages
cream cheese, at
room temperature

2 tablespoons
mayonnaise

½ teaspoon salt

8 slices
pumpernickel bread

1. Use a box grater to grate the seeded cucumber. Place the grated cucumber in a colander over a bowl and let it drain. Using a clean kitchen towel or paper towels, squeeze out the excess moisture. Set aside.

2. Place the scallions in a food processor and process until finely chopped. Add the grated cucumber and process again for 30 seconds. Add the cream cheese, mayonnaise, and salt. Process until smooth.

3. To assemble the sandwiches, divide the cream cheese mixture evenly between 4 slices of bread. Layer the cucumber slices over the top of the mixture, then cover with the remaining 4 slices of bread and press down firmly. Cut away the crusts. Halve the sandwiches diagonally and then diagonally again, to make triangles. Serve immediately.

INGREDIENT TIP: The spread on these sandwiches is based on Benedictine, a classic recipe from my home of Louisville, Kentucky. Try serving the spread at a Kentucky Derby party for a regional flair.

APPLE CHEDDAR GRILLED CHEESE

NUT-FREE, ONE-POT, UNDER 30 MINUTES

Serves 4   **Prep time:** 5 minutes   **Cook time:** 10 minutes

This Apple Cheddar Grilled Cheese is a prime example of why the 5-ingredient method works so well. What more do you need than hearty bread, sharp white Cheddar, tart apples, luscious butter, and a pop of whole-grain mustard to bring it all together? Each ingredient has its own role to ensure that you have the most balanced eating experience possible. Grab that bowl of Tortellini Tomato Soup (page 47) and get dunking.

8 thick slices multi-grain bread

1 tablespoon whole-grain mustard

12 slices white Cheddar cheese

2 green apples, unpeeled, cored, and thinly sliced

4 tablespoons unsalted butter, softened

1. Spread a thin layer of whole-grain mustard on 4 slices of bread. Top each slice with 2 slices of cheese, an equal amount of apple slices, a third slice of cheese, and a slice of bread. Press down lightly. Spread the softened butter on both outer sides of the bread.

2. In a large skillet over medium-low heat, cook the sandwiches for 3 to 5 minutes, until the bread toasts and the cheese is slightly melted. Flip, and cook for about 3 minutes more, until both sides are golden brown and the cheese is melted. Keep an eye on them to make sure the outside isn't getting too toasted before the cheese melts. If so, reduce the heat to low and cover with a lid until the cheese is gooey. Serve warm.

CAPRESE PANINI

ONE-POT, UNDER 30 MINUTES

Serves 4   **Prep time:** 5 minutes   **Cook time:** 10 minutes

One of my favorite meals on planet Earth is a Caprese salad. Plop that between two pieces of crusty sourdough bread and it's guaranteed to make my day and probably yours, as well. If you've already made the staples from chapter 7, then you'll have two of the ingredients needed for this recipe on hand. I love eating this with a handful of salt and vinegar chips for the perfect work lunch pick-me-up.

8 slices
sourdough bread

Simple Pesto
(page 106), or
store-bought

2 large
tomatoes, sliced

16 ounces mozzarella
cheese, sliced

Balsamic Glaze
(page 105), for
drizzling

3 tablespoons olive oil

1. Spread a thin layer of pesto on 4 slices of bread. Top each slice with a quarter of the tomato slices and a quarter of the mozzarella slices. Drizzle the mozzarella with the glaze and top with the remaining 4 slices of bread. Press down lightly. Brush the olive oil on both outer sides of the bread.

2. Place the sandwiches in a large skillet or grill pan over medium-low heat. Put a heavy skillet on top to press down the sandwiches and cook for 3 to 5 minutes, until the bread toasts and the cheese is slightly melted. Flip and cook for about 3 minutes more, until both sides are golden brown and the cheese is melted. Keep an eye on them to make sure the outside isn't getting too toasted before the cheese melts. If so, reduce heat to low and cover with a lid until the cheese is gooey. Serve warm.

BBQ TOFU AND PINEAPPLE SAMMIES

DAIRY-FREE, NUT-FREE, ONE-POT

Serves 4   **Prep time:** 20 minutes   **Cook time:** 35 minutes

Every time someone tells me they don't like tofu, I respectfully suggest to them that they may be cooking it wrong. I spill some of those cooking secrets in this recipe, but it also doesn't hurt that barbecue sauce and tofu are a perfect match. Add in roasted pineapple, red onion, and a fluffy Hawaiian bun and you're in for serious bliss. Now, go forth and allow this sweet and savory sammie to blow your mind.

1 (15-ounce) block extra-firm tofu

½ teaspoon salt

¼ teaspoon freshly ground black pepper

1½ tablespoons olive oil

4 (½-inch-thick) pineapple rings, canned or fresh

¼ cup Honey Mustard Barbecue Sauce (page 103)

4 Hawaiian hamburger buns, sliced (and toasted if desired)

½ cup red onion, thinly sliced

1. Preheat the oven to 425°F.

2. While the oven preheats, wrap the tofu in a few layers of paper towels or a clean kitchen towel and set it on a cutting board. Place a heavy cast-iron skillet or Dutch oven on top of the wrapped tofu and let sit for 10 minutes. Pat dry the drained tofu and tear into rough, bite-size pieces. Don't use a knife for this because the more irregular the edges, the crispier the tofu will get.

3. In a medium bowl, toss the tofu pieces with the salt, pepper, and oil to coat. Scatter the tofu on two thirds of a baking sheet, making sure the pieces don't touch. Add the pineapple rings to the remainder of the baking sheet and bake 30 to 35 minutes, stirring the tofu and flipping the pineapple halfway through.

CONTINUED →

4. Toss the tofu with the barbecue sauce to coat. To build your sammie, start with the bottom half of 1 Hawaiian bun, pile on the tofu, red onion, and a ring of pineapple. Close the sammie with the top half of the bun. Repeat with the remaining buns and ingredients and serve.

INGREDIENT TIP: If you're not freezing your tofu, you need to be. Freezing allows all the excess moisture to escape the tofu once it's thawed, which means extra crispy and delicious tofu every time. If you combine freezing with pressing your tofu, you'll never turn your nose up at it again.

PHILLY CHEESE PORTOBELLO SUBS

NUT-FREE, ONE-POT, UNDER 30 MINUTES

Serves 4   **Prep time:** 10 minutes   **Cook time:** 20 minutes

The Philly cheesesteak is a classic sandwich, and for good reason. This vegefied version uses beefy portobello mushrooms so you don't miss the steak whatsoever, as well as the go-to toppings of peppers and onion. Simplicity is key here, but if you require a moist-maker on a sandwich, as I do, I highly recommend slathering your toasted hoagies with Garlic Aioli (page 107).

1 tablespoon olive oil

1 yellow onion, thinly sliced

1 green bell pepper, thinly sliced

1 pound portobello mushrooms, thinly sliced

½ teaspoon salt

½ teaspoon freshly ground black pepper

8 slices provolone cheese

4 hoagie rolls, halved lengthwise and lightly toasted

1. Heat the oil in a large skillet over medium-high heat. Add the sliced onion and bell pepper and sauté for about 5 minutes, until they begin to soften. Add the sliced portobellos and continue to sauté for about 12 minutes, until the mushrooms are browned. Season with the salt and black pepper.

2. Divide the mixture into four even portions in the skillet and top each with 2 slices of provolone. Turn off the heat and cover to allow the cheese to melt.

3. Using a large spatula, transfer the cheese-covered filling portions to each toasted hoagie. Serve warm.

VARIATION TIP: If you're on team Cheez Whiz when it comes to your Philly cheesesteak sandwich, feel free to swap the provolone for about 1.5 ounces of the yellow stuff per sub.

HARVEST APPLE SLAW

GLUTEN-FREE, NUT-FREE, ONE-POT

Serves 4   **Prep time:** 10 minutes, plus 1 hour to chill

Slaw is one of those controversial dishes that you probably either love or hate. If you've previously found yourself disliking it, give this recipe a try. This cabbage-free slaw uses a base of shredded apples and carrots. It's tart and slightly sweet, and has a pretty epic crunch factor. This one is great as a quick side, potluck dish, spring roll filling, or topping for the BBQ Tofu and Pineapple Sammies (page 53) in place of the pineapple.

½ cup plain
Greek yogurt

2 tablespoons apple
cider vinegar

1 tablespoon
maple syrup

½ teaspoon salt

½ teaspoon freshly
ground black pepper

2 green apples,
unpeeled, cored and
shredded

1 cup shredded
carrots

In a large bowl, whisk together the Greek yogurt, vinegar, maple syrup, salt, and pepper. Toss with the shredded apples and carrots. Allow the slaw to chill in the refrigerator for at least 1 hour before serving.

INGREDIENT TIP: This slaw can be made with many shredded vegetables. I love using red or green cabbage, beets, or even sliced celery. If you have dried cranberries or raisins on hand, those are also great additions, along with toasted nuts. You can also swap the Greek yogurt for mayonnaise, if desired.

BUFFALO CAULIFLOWER AND CELERY SALAD

GLUTEN-FREE, NUT-FREE, ONE-POT

Serves 4　　**Prep time:** 10 minutes, plus 20 minutes to cool
Cook time: 10 minutes

Tailgates and parties don't have to be polarizing affairs for vegetarians. There will surely be more than enough wing platters to go around, but you'll have this crunchy and spicy salad to call your own. Nothing screams game day more than buffalo sauce, blue cheese, and celery! Pair it with Loaded Sweet Potato Fries (page 70) and you'll have a meal fit for any hungry sports fan.

1 medium cauliflower head, cut into small florets

½ teaspoon salt

½ cup Greek Yogurt Cucumber Ranch (page 104)

¼ cup buffalo sauce

8 celery stalks, cut at an angle into ¼-inch-thick pieces

⅓ cup crumbled blue cheese

½ teaspoon freshly ground black pepper

1. Bring a medium pot of water to a boil over high heat, and add the cauliflower florets and salt. Simmer on medium heat for 3 to 5 minutes. Drain, transfer the florets to a large bowl, and set aside to cool for 15 minutes.

2. In a medium bowl, whisk together the cucumber ranch and the buffalo sauce.

3. Once the cauliflower has cooled to room temperature, toss it with the sauce, celery, and blue cheese. Season with the pepper and serve at room temperature or chilled.

INGREDIENT TIP: Celery is notorious for having stringy fibers along the back that can make it hard to bite and chop. Use a vegetable peeler to get rid of those tough fibers before chopping the celery.

BUTTER BEAN SALAD MELT

NUT-FREE, ONE-POT, UNDER 30 MINUTES

Serves 4   **Prep time:** 10 minutes   **Cook time:** 10 minutes

As the name suggests, butter beans (aka lima beans) possess a buttery texture that's delicious in so many dishes. They're an underrated legume, as lima beans are packed with protein and fiber like most beans, plus they provide a ton of iron, which isn't easy to come by in plant foods. But now's their time to shine—they add such a lovely texture and flavor to this vegetarian spin on a tuna melt that you may start keeping them on hand.

2 (16-ounce) cans butter beans, drained and rinsed

5 tablespoons Garlic Aioli (page 107)

1 celery stalk, minced

½ teaspoon salt

4 large sourdough bread slices

1½ cups shredded Cheddar cheese

1. Preheat the oven to 375°F.

2. In a large bowl, mash the butter beans thoroughly. Add the Garlic Aioli, celery, and salt to the bowl. Mash all the ingredients together until well combined.

3. Place the sourdough slices on a baking sheet and toast in the preheated oven for about 3 minutes, until lightly golden.

4. Remove the toasts from the oven and pile each slice evenly with the butter bean salad. Top each with a quarter of the shredded cheese and return them to the oven. Bake for about 5 minutes, until the cheese is melted. Serve warm.

NO-MAYO POTATO SALAD

DAIRY-FREE, GLUTEN-FREE, NUT-FREE, ONE-POT, VEGAN

Serves 4   **Prep time:** 10 minutes, plus 10 minutes to chill
Cook time: 25 minutes

What summer cookout is complete without potato salad? This time, ditch the mayo and opt for this lighter version that you won't have to worry about serving outside. Bonus: This salad is even better the next day and will last up to five days in an airtight container in the refrigerator. Be sure to remove it about 30 minutes before serving to allow the vinaigrette to loosen up and recoat the potatoes.

1 pound baby Yukon Gold potatoes

1½ teaspoons salt, divided

1 garlic clove, finely minced

2 tablespoons Dijon mustard

2 tablespoons white wine vinegar

¼ cup olive oil

¼ teaspoon freshly ground black pepper

¼ cup freshly chopped dill

1. Place the potatoes in a large pot or Dutch oven with enough water to cover them by an inch. Add 1 teaspoon of salt and bring the water to a boil over high heat. Cover, reduce the heat to medium-high, and simmer for 15 to 20 minutes, depending on the size of your potatoes, until fork-tender. Drain the potatoes and set them aside to dry slightly.

2. While the potatoes are cooling, make the vinaigrette: In a large bowl, combine the garlic, Dijon, and vinegar. Slowly stream in the olive oil, whisking constantly, until fully combined and emulsified. Season with the remaining ½ teaspoon of salt and the pepper.

3. Add the dill to the bowl with the vinaigrette and add the potatoes. Toss well and let chill in the refrigerator for at least 10 minutes before serving.

   INGREDIENT TIP: If you already have a sack of russet potatoes in your pantry, don't ignore them! Just wash, peel, and cube into one-inch pieces before boiling.

ROASTED SWEET
POTATOES WITH TAHINI,
POMEGRANATE, AND
FETA, PAGE 71

CHAPTER FIVE

Hearty Mains

CHICKPEA COCONUT CURRY

Serves 6   **Prep time:** 5 minutes   **Cook time:** 15 minutes

As someone who is consistently developing new recipes and experimenting in the kitchen, I rarely make the same dish over and over again. One major exception is this chickpea coconut curry. Since it's made up of pantry staples, I make sure I never run out of anything so I can make it whenever I want. I serve mine over basmati rice and topped with fresh cilantro, lime, and warm naan.

1 tablespoon olive oil

2 teaspoons curry powder

1 (15-ounce) can crushed tomatoes

1 (13.5-ounce) can coconut milk

2 (15-ounce) cans chickpeas, drained and rinsed

½ teaspoon salt

¼ teaspoon freshly ground black pepper

Basmati rice, prepared according to package directions, for serving

1. Heat the oil in a large pot or Dutch oven over medium heat. Add the curry powder and stir for about 1 minute, until toasted. Add the crushed tomatoes and gently stir.

2. Add the coconut milk and chickpeas. Stir and reduce the heat to low. Simmer, stirring occasionally, for about 10 minutes, until the sauce is thickened and the chickpeas are slightly softened. Season with the salt and pepper.

3. Spoon the chickpea coconut curry over the prepared rice and serve.

MAKE-AHEAD TIP: This curry will keep for up to three days in an airtight container in the refrigerator. To freeze, allow the chickpeas to cool completely before transferring them to a freezer bag. Lay flat in the freezer for up to three months.

QUINOA STUFFED PEPPERS

FREEZER-FRIENDLY, GLUTEN-FREE, NUT-FREE, ONE-POT
Serves 6   **Prep time:** 15 minutes   **Cook time:** 40 minutes

Growing up, I always got so excited when stuffed peppers were on the menu. Being able to eat the element that your dinner is served in is a novel idea that would get anyone excited. I mean, look at bread bowls! These stuffed peppers are perfect for meal prep and will keep you full all afternoon. For some added healthy fats, top them with a spoonful of guacamole or Greek yogurt.

4 cups uncooked quinoa

1 (14.5-ounce) can fire-roasted diced tomatoes and green chiles

1 (15.5-ounce) can black beans, drained and rinsed

1½ cups shredded Cheddar cheese, divided

½ teaspoon salt

¼ teaspoon freshly ground black pepper

6 large bell peppers, tops and ribs removed

1. Preheat the oven to 400°F.

2. In a medium pot, cook the quinoa according to package directions.

3. In a large bowl, combine the quinoa, tomatoes and green chiles, black beans, ½ cup of shredded cheese, the salt, and black pepper. Mix to incorporate.

4. Place the bell peppers in a 9-by-9-inch baking dish. If necessary, slice a sliver off the bottoms of the bell peppers to make sure they can stand upright. Scoop 1 cup of the quinoa mixture into each bell pepper. Top the bell peppers with the remaining 1 cup of shredded cheese.

5. Cover the baking dish with aluminum foil and bake for 30 minutes. Remove the foil and bake for about 10 minutes more, or until the cheese is bubbling and golden brown. Remove the stuffed peppers from the oven and serve warm.

INGREDIENT TIP: Microwavable quinoa and rice are lifesavers on busy weeknights. You can buy both of them in shelf-stable pouches as well as frozen in steamer bags.

LENTIL BURRITO BOWLS

DAIRY-FREE, GLUTEN-FREE, NUT-FREE, ONE-POT, UNDER 30 MINUTES, VEGAN
Serves 4   **Prep time:** 10 minutes   **Cook time:** 15 minutes

Everyone's burrito bowl order is extremely personal. Mine tends to change from season to season, but there are always a few constant toppings, particularly corn and avocado. Since most restaurants don't offer lentils as a burrito option yet, I'll be making mine at home for the foreseeable future. If you're anything like me, you'll want a bag of tortilla chips close by so you can scoop all this goodness up.

2 cups split red lentils

3 teaspoons taco seasoning

½ teaspoon salt

¼ teaspoon freshly ground black pepper

4 cups shredded romaine lettuce

2 avocados, peeled, pitted, and thinly sliced

1 cup frozen corn, thawed

1. In a medium pot, prepare the lentils according to package directions. Once tender, stir in the taco seasoning, salt, and pepper.

2. Build the bowls by layering the lentil taco mix, shredded romaine, avocado, and corn. Enjoy chilled or warm.

VARIATION TIP: Since everyone's bowl is a personal thing, why not put out bowls of ingredients so everyone can assemble their own? Whether you follow this recipe or use a variety of ingredients you've got on hand (think leftovers!), the whole family will enjoy being in charge of their own bowl domain.

EGGPLANT PARMESAN ROULADES

FREEZER-FRIENDLY, GLUTEN-FREE, NUT-FREE

Serves 6   **Prep time:** 30 minutes   **Cook time:** 40 minutes

Italian cuisine is such a delicious comfort food genre and the perfect go-to for entertaining. Even if you're feeding meat eaters, they'll appreciate this lasagna-like dish that's hearty and full of flavor. If you want a fail-safe way to impress any guest, serve these roulades with a vegan Caesar salad and a fresh baguette with Simple Pesto (page 106). *Chef's Kiss*

2 medium eggplants, peeled and cut lengthwise into ¼-inch slices

1 teaspoon salt

2 cups full-fat ricotta cheese

1 cup grated mozzarella cheese

1 cup grated Parmesan cheese, divided

1 teaspoon freshly ground black pepper

1 cup marinara sauce

1. Preheat the oven to 400°F.

2. Spread the eggplant slices on a baking sheet lined with paper towels. Sprinkle the eggplant with salt on both sides and let them sit for 20 minutes to draw out the excess moisture. Pat dry thoroughly with a paper towel.

3. Remove the paper towels and bake the eggplant on the same baking sheet for about 15 minutes, until soft. Remove the eggplant from the oven and allow to cool slightly.

4. In a medium bowl, mix together the ricotta, mozzarella, ½ cup of Parmesan, and the pepper.

5. Spread a spoonful of the cheese mixture onto each eggplant slice, then roll it up. Repeat with the remaining eggplant slices and filling.

6. In a 13-by-9-inch baking dish, spread ½ cup marinara sauce over the bottom, then add all the roll-ups, seam-side down. Pour the remaining ½ cup marinara sauce over the roll-ups and top them with the remaining ½ cup of Parmesan.

7. Bake for about 25 minutes, or until the cheese is melted and golden brown.

WHOLE LEMON-ROASTED CAULIFLOWER

DAIRY-FREE, GLUTEN-FREE, NUT-FREE, ONE-POT, VEGAN

Serves 4   **Prep time:** 10 minutes   **Cook time:** 1 hour

Vegetarians tend to get the short end of the stick when it comes to show-stopping main dishes. Think about every time you've seen an omnivore gasp at a rack of lamb or a pot roast as it's brought to the table. Vegetarians get to eat amazingly delicious grub, too, and now, with this whole roasted cauliflower, you get to gawk at your beautiful meal, as well.

1 (2-pound) medium cauliflower head, leaves and bottom stem discarded

½ cup tahini

½ cup warm water

2 garlic cloves, finely minced

¼ cup lemon juice

1 tablespoon lemon zest

¾ teaspoon salt

½ teaspoon smoked paprika

1. Preheat the oven to 375°F. Line a Dutch oven with parchment paper and place the cauliflower in the middle.

2. In a medium bowl, whisk together the tahini, warm water, garlic, lemon juice, lemon zest, salt, and paprika. Drizzle just enough of the tahini sauce to completely coat the cauliflower, and brush evenly all over the cauliflower.

3. Cover with a lid and bake for 25 minutes. Remove the lid and bake for another 20 to 30 minutes, or until a knife is easily inserted through the center.

4. Drizzle more tahini sauce over the cauliflower and cut it into wedges. Serve with additional tahini sauce at the table.

TERIYAKI CAULIFLOWER

DAIRY-FREE, FREEZER-FRIENDLY, GLUTEN-FREE, NUT-FREE, ONE-POT, VEGAN

Serves 4   **Prep time:** 10 minutes   **Cook time:** 40 minutes

I don't like referring to saucy-roasted cauliflower florets as "wings." Sure, they use a similar cooking application as chicken wings, and they hit similar notes when you eat them, but I think cauliflower deserves its own platform. Cauliflower doesn't have to mimic something else to get anyone to like it. It's perfect as it is, and this teriyaki cauliflower is a prime example of that perfection.

1 (2-pound) medium cauliflower head, leaves and bottom stem discarded

2 tablespoons olive oil

½ teaspoon salt

1 cup teriyaki sauce, divided

4 scallions, white and green parts, thinly sliced

2 tablespoons toasted sesame seeds

1 red Fresno chile, thinly sliced

1. Preheat the oven to 425°F.

2. Cut the cauliflower into small florets. On a baking sheet, toss the cauliflower with the oil and salt and spread it out evenly. Bake for 30 minutes, tossing halfway through.

3. Remove the cauliflower from the oven and brush it with ½ cup of teriyaki sauce. Return it to the oven and bake for about 10 minutes, until the cauliflower is caramelized.

4. Toss the cauliflower with the remaining ½ cup of teriyaki sauce, and top it with the scallions, sesame seeds, and sliced chile before serving.

SWEET CHILI TOFU BROCCOLI STIR-FRY

DAIRY-FREE, FREEZER-FRIENDLY, GLUTEN-FREE, NUT-FREE, ONE-POT, VEGAN
Serves 4   **Prep time:** 20 minutes   **Cook time:** 20 minutes

It can be tricky ordering takeout as a vegetarian. Sometimes, you'll see a dish that seems perfectly vegetarian-friendly, only to read closer and find out it was prepared with or alongside meat. Avoid cross-contamination by making this simple and mouthwatering stir-fry. I like serving this with plain steamed rice.

1 (15-ounce) block extra-firm tofu

½ teaspoon salt

2 tablespoons cornstarch

2 tablespoons olive oil

2 scallions, white and green parts, sliced

½ cup broccoli florets

1 cup sweet chili sauce

1. Wrap the tofu in a few layers of paper towels or a clean kitchen towel and set it on a cutting board. Place a heavy cast-iron skillet or Dutch oven on top of the wrapped tofu and let it sit for 10 minutes. Pat dry the drained tofu, then dice it into 1-inch cubes. Sprinkle the salt and cornstarch on the tofu cubes and toss well.

2. Heat the oil in a large pan over medium-high heat. Sauté the tofu for about 10 minutes, until crisp and golden on all sides. Transfer the tofu to a plate.

3. In the same large pan, combine the scallions and broccoli, adding a bit more oil if needed. Sauté the vegetables for about 5 minutes, until the broccoli starts to become tender.

4. Add the sweet chili sauce to the pan and bring to a simmer. Reduce the heat to medium and add the tofu back in. Allow to simmer for about 2 more minutes, until the sauce thickens and the tofu is coated. Serve.

INGREDIENT TIP: If you have a sensitivity to corn starch, arrowroot powder will have the same effect.

PARMESAN-GARLIC STUFFED PORTOBELLO MUSHROOMS

NUT-FREE, ONE-POT, UNDER 30 MINUTES

Serves 4 **Prep time:** 10 minutes **Cook time:** 20 minutes

Portobello mushrooms are one of my favorite vegetarian ingredients. They're thick and hearty enough to take on marinades, much like meat, and they act as the perfect vehicle for a myriad of fillings. This appetizer-turned-main-course is amazing, both when served alone and as part of a big Italian spread. Pair these with the Eggplant Parmesan Roulades (page 65) and Pesto Pasta Salad (page 95) to complete your family-style dinner.

4 portobello mushrooms

4 tablespoons olive oil, divided

10 ounces frozen chopped spinach, thawed and excess water removed

½ cup grated Parmesan cheese, divided

3 garlic cloves, finely minced

¼ teaspoon salt

¼ teaspoon freshly ground black pepper

⅓ cup Italian bread crumbs

1. Preheat the oven to 400°F.

2. Remove the stems from the mushrooms and use a spoon to scoop out the gills. Wipe the mushrooms down with a wet paper towel. Rub the mushrooms on all sides with 2 tablespoons of oil, and arrange them, cap-side down, on a baking sheet.

3. In a medium bowl, prepare the filling: Combine the remaining 2 tablespoons of oil with the spinach, ¼ cup of Parmesan, the garlic, salt, and pepper. Divide the filling evenly between the mushrooms.

4. In a small bowl, prepare the topping: Toss together the remaining ¼ cup of Parmesan and the bread crumbs. Divide the topping evenly between the mushrooms.

5. Bake for about 20 minutes, or until the mushrooms become dark brown and are just tender. Serve warm.

LOADED SWEET POTATO FRIES

FREEZER-FRIENDLY, GLUTEN-FREE, NUT-FREE, ONE-POT

Serves 4   **Prep time:** 5 minutes   **Cook time:** 30 minutes

The only thing better than sweet potato fries? Loaded sweet potato fries. Whether you go for shoestring, crinkle cut, or waffle, these fries will have the whole family gobbling up every last morsel. And it doesn't matter if you're vegetarian or not; there's nothing like a crispy sweet potato dripping in toppings. These loaded fries are a perfect match with BBQ Tofu and Pineapple Sammies (page 53) and Quick Blender Salsa (page 31) for game day.

2 pounds frozen sweet potato fries

1 cup frozen corn

½ teaspoon salt

¼ teaspoon freshly ground black pepper

1 cup shredded Cheddar cheese

½ cup Greek Yogurt Cucumber Ranch (page 104)

½ cup guacamole

1. Preheat the oven to 425°F.

2. Combine the sweet potato fries and frozen corn and spread them in a single layer on 2 baking sheets. Bake for 20 minutes, tossing halfway through. Season with the salt and pepper.

3. Layer the fries and corn with the cheese and bake for another 7 to 8 minutes, or until the cheese is melted.

4. Remove the loaded fries from the oven and top them with the cucumber ranch and guacamole. Serve warm.

INGREDIENT TIP: Sweet potato fries are super easy to make from scratch at home. Peel the sweet potatoes and slice them into quarter-inch-thick planks, and then into long, thin quarter-inch fries. Bake them on a greased or nonstick baking sheet for 25 minutes. Add the salt, pepper, and cheese, and then bake them for the remaining time.

ROASTED SWEET POTATOES WITH TAHINI, POMEGRANATE, AND FETA

FREEZER-FRIENDLY, GLUTEN-FREE, NUT-FREE, ONE-POT

Serves 4   **Prep time:** 10 minutes   **Cook time:** 1 hour

One of my best friends, who was a vegetarian for years, frequently complained to me about how tired she was of eating sweet potatoes, being that they're one of the heartier veggie-based mains that are frequently offered. I feel that, and I love dreaming up ways that I can make plant-centric food fun again. These stuffed sweet potatoes contain everything from creamy tahini and spicy crispy chickpeas to tangy feta cheese and a juicy pop from the pomegranate. You won't tire of these flavorful sweet potatoes, pinky promise.

4 medium sweet potatoes, scrubbed and dried

1 tablespoon olive oil

½ teaspoon salt

¼ teaspoon freshly ground black pepper

2 cups Crispy Chipotle Chickpeas (page 36)

¼ cup tahini

½ cup pomegranate arils

½ cup crumbled feta

1. Preheat the oven to 375°F.

2. Prick the sweet potatoes all over with a fork and place them on a baking sheet. Rub the potatoes all over with the oil and roast for 45 to 55 minutes, until just tender. Let cool for 5 to 10 minutes before slitting the tops and lightly mashing the insides with a fork. Season the flesh with the salt and pepper.

3. Fill each of the sweet potatoes with the chickpeas. Drizzle them with the tahini, top them with the pomegranate arils and feta, and serve.

MAKE-AHEAD TIP: These sweet potatoes are perfect for meal prepping for lunches throughout the week. I recommend storing the baked sweet potatoes and toppings separately. Everything will keep for four or five days in an airtight container in the refrigerator.

BROCCOLI CHEDDAR
BAKED POTATOES

FREEZER-FRIENDLY, GLUTEN-FREE, NUT-FREE, ONE-POT

Serves 4   **Prep time:** 15 minutes   **Cook time:** 1 hour 20 minutes

Nothing relieves the soul more than a baked potato filled to the brim with broccoli and cheese. If plain potatoes aren't your jam, then this healthier take on a classic will be your new go-to. To save time in a pinch, try cooking your potatoes in the microwave before stuffing them. Simply prick the potatoes all over with a fork and microwave them for five minutes on each side. Then, you can slit them open and fill them as you like.

4 medium russet potatoes, scrubbed and dried

1 teaspoon olive oil

4 tablespoons salted butter, softened

2 cups shredded Cheddar cheese, divided

1½ cups chopped cooked broccoli

½ cup Greek yogurt

½ teaspoon salt

½ teaspoon freshly ground black pepper

1. Preheat the oven to 375°F.

2. Prick the potatoes all over with a fork and place them on a baking sheet. Rub the potatoes all over with the oil and roast for 45 to 55 minutes, until just tender. Let cool for 5 to 10 minutes before slitting the tops and lightly mashing the insides with a fork. Add 1 tablespoon of the salted butter to the cavity of each potato.

3. In a medium bowl, mix ¾ cup of Cheddar with the broccoli, Greek yogurt, salt, and pepper.

4. Divide the filling evenly among the potatoes, then top them with the remaining 1¼ cups of Cheddar. Bake for about 20 minutes, until the cheese is melted and the potatoes are heated through.

CREAMY POLENTA WITH ROASTED BEETS

FREEZER-FRIENDLY, GLUTEN-FREE, NUT-FREE

Serves 4   **Prep time:** 10 minutes   **Cook time:** 40 minutes

If you're stuck in a date night rut, this elegant and delicious meal will snap you out of it in a hurry. The simplistic flavors of earthy beets and polenta, tangy goat cheese, and sweet balsamic glaze enhance one another enough to deliver restaurant-level sophistication to your own home. Add a sprinkle of chopped parsley for a pop of color. For dessert, follow this dish with Yogurt Panna Cotta (page 99) or Lava Cake (page 102) to ease that sweet tooth and cap off the night with a bang.

3 large beets, peeled, root and tops discarded, and cut into 1-inch cubes

1 tablespoon olive oil, plus more for drizzling

1½ teaspoons salt, divided

½ teaspoon freshly ground black pepper

3 cups water

1 cup polenta

2 garlic cloves, finely minced

8 ounces goat cheese, divided

Balsamic Glaze (page 105), for drizzling

1. Preheat the oven to 400°F. Line a baking sheet with aluminum foil or parchment paper.

2. Place the beets on the prepared baking sheet. Toss them with the oil, 1 teaspoon of salt, and the pepper. Roast for 35 to 40 minutes, turning halfway through, until the beets are fork-tender.

3. Meanwhile, make the polenta: In a medium pot, bring the water to a boil over high heat. Add the polenta and garlic and whisk until smooth. Reduce the heat to low and simmer for about 15 minutes, or until the polenta is thickened. Add 4 ounces of goat cheese and the remaining ½ teaspoon of salt and stir until smooth.

4. Ladle the polenta into shallow bowls and top them with the roasted beets. Crumble the remaining 4 ounces of goat cheese over the top and finish with a drizzle of Balsamic Glaze and olive oil, if desired. Serve warm.

CAJUN RICE SKILLET

DAIRY-FREE, GLUTEN-FREE, FREEZER-FRIENDLY, NUT-FREE, VEGAN
Serves 4   **Prep time:** 10 minutes   **Cook time:** 35 minutes

Spice up your life with this Creole-inspired rice skillet that boasts a healthy dose of okra. Okra is a flowering plant that's rich in many nutrients and packed with vitamins C and K. It even provides plant protein, which is both unique for a vegetable and essential for vegetarians. I love the flavor it adds to this meal and, when cooked properly, the texture is nothing to be worried about.

3 cups water

1½ cups uncooked white rice

2 tablespoons olive oil

1 (12-ounce) package frozen sliced okra, thawed

1 large green bell pepper, chopped

1 cup frozen corn, thawed

1 tablespoon Cajun seasoning

1 teaspoon salt

½ teaspoon freshly ground black pepper

1. In a large saucepan over medium-high heat, combine the water and rice. Once the water comes to a boil, reduce the heat to low, cover, and cook for about 15 minutes, or until all the water is absorbed. Set aside.

2. Heat the oil in a large skillet over medium heat. Add the okra, bell pepper, and corn and sauté for about 5 minutes, until the vegetables are tender. Season with the Cajun seasoning, salt, and black pepper.

3. Add the rice to the skillet and stir to combine. Continue to cook, stirring frequently, for about 10 minutes, until the rice is toasted. Serve warm.

MAKE-AHEAD TIP: This dish freezes well for future dinner "emergencies." Spoon individual portions into freezer bags and lay them flat to freeze for up to six months. This dish can also be refrigerated in an airtight container for up to three days.

MUSHROOM AND BRUSSELS SPROUT PIZZA

FREEZER-FRIENDLY, NUT-FREE, ONE-POT, UNDER 30 MINUTES

Serves 4 **Prep time:** 15 minutes **Cook time:** 15 minutes

Two of my favorite vegetables are mushrooms and Brussels sprouts. The reason why I love them so much could also be the reason so many people claim to dislike them: it's all in the way they're cooked. My advice? Throw them on a pizza.

1 tablespoon olive oil, plus more for greasing

1 cup shredded Brussels sprouts

4 ounces baby bella mushrooms, sliced

½ teaspoon salt

¼ teaspoon freshly ground black pepper

1 (8-ounce) package pizza dough, at room temperature

2 cups shredded Gouda

Balsamic Glaze (page 105), for drizzling

1. Preheat the oven to 450°F. Grease a baking sheet with olive oil.

2. In a large bowl, toss together the olive oil, Brussels sprouts, mushrooms, salt, and pepper.

3. On the prepared baking sheet, roll out the pizza dough to a 10- to 12-inch circle.

4. Evenly scatter half of the Brussels sprouts and mushrooms over the dough. Add all the shredded Gouda in an even layer, then scatter the rest of the Brussels sprouts and mushrooms over the cheese.

5. Bake for 10 to 15 minutes, until the crust is golden and the cheese is melted. Drizzle the pizza with the glaze to serve.

COOKING TIP: To freeze, line your baking sheet with aluminum foil, then proceed as directed through step 4. Only bake for seven minutes, then allow it to cool completely. Transfer the pizza to a plate and wrap it in several layers of plastic wrap and foil. The pizza can be frozen for up to three months. When you're ready, bake the frozen pizza for 10 to 15 minutes and finish with the glaze.

TOMATO GALETTE

NUT-FREE, ONE-POT

Serves 6 **Prep time:** 15 minutes, plus 15 minutes to chill **Cook time:** 55 minutes

Any excuse I can use to have pie for dinner, I'm all in. This tomato galette is perfect for those late summer evenings when you still have the best tomatoes that the season has to offer, but it's cool enough to start cooking with your oven again. For a fun, Caprese twist, swap shredded mozzarella for the Cheddar and serve with Balsamic Glaze (page 105).

1 single pie crust, store-bought or homemade

3 to 4 medium heirloom tomatoes, thinly sliced

½ teaspoon salt

¼ teaspoon freshly ground black pepper

3 cups shredded Cheddar cheese

1 egg, beaten

¼ cup thinly sliced fresh basil

1. Line a baking sheet with parchment paper. If using store-bought pie crust, place the pie crust on the prepared baking sheet. If homemade, on a floured work surface, roll out the dough to about ⅛-inch thickness. Transfer the pie dough to the prepared baking sheet.

2. Layer the tomatoes over the center of the pie dough, leaving a 3-inch border around the edges. Season the tomatoes with the salt and pepper and sprinkle the cheese evenly over the tomatoes. Fold the outside edges of dough over the outermost tomatoes. Brush the crust with the beaten egg. Chill the galette in the refrigerator for at least 15 minutes, or until ready to bake.

3. Meanwhile, preheat the oven to 375°F. Bake the galette for 45 to 55 minutes, until the crust is golden brown. Let cool for 5 minutes, then top it with the sliced basil. Serve warm.

INGREDIENT TIP: If your tomatoes look extra juicy once they're sliced, lay them on a layer of paper towels. Salt them and wait a few minutes while the salt draws out the moisture. Use additional paper towels to soak up the excess liquid.

CREAMY COCONUT
VERMICELLI,
PAGE 90

CHAPTER SIX

Pasta and Noodles

SPINACH MACARONI AND CHEESE

FREEZER-FRIENDLY, NUT-FREE

Serves 4   **Prep time:** 10 minutes   **Cook time:** 25 minutes

Macaroni and cheese is a weeknight staple that the whole family flips for. Since you know there's nothing that could stop the crew from eating it, you might as well throw in some vitamin-rich spinach while you're at it. I love using mac and cheese as an emergency dinner because I can generally substitute whatever cheese I have on hand and swap out regular pasta for protein-packed chickpea pasta or gluten-free pasta when I need it.

1 (16-ounce) package elbow noodles

1 cup heavy (whipping) cream

1¾ cups shredded Monterey Jack cheese

½ teaspoon salt

½ teaspoon freshly ground black pepper

¼ teaspoon mustard powder

10 ounces frozen chopped spinach, defrosted and excess water removed

1. Bring a large pot of water to a boil over high heat. Add the pasta and cook according to package directions. Drain and set aside.

2. Meanwhile, heat the cream in a large saucepan or cast-iron skillet over medium heat until it just begins to bubble. Add the cheese, salt, pepper, and mustard powder. Whisk the cheese sauce for 5 to 7 minutes, until bubbly and the cheese is melted.

3. Add the cooked elbow noodles to the cheese sauce and stir until coated. Stir in the defrosted spinach until well combined. Cook for 2 to 3 minutes more, until the spinach is heated through. Serve warm.

INGREDIENT TIP: Looking for extra creamy macaroni and cheese? Simply shred your cheese by hand instead of buying it pre-shredded. Shredded cheese in a bag contains preservatives and anti-clumping agents meant to keep the cheese from clumping together in the bag, which can lead to a grittier texture and difficulty melting.

CHEESY BAKED RAVIOLI

FREEZER-FRIENDLY, NUT-FREE, ONE-POT

Serves 6   **Prep time:** 10 minutes   **Cook time:** 25 minutes

Lasagna is great and all, but it has a reputation for being quite the labor of love. A quick weeknight alternative is this cheesy baked ravioli that hits all of the same notes in a fraction of the time. There's no need to boil the ravioli since it cooks perfectly in the oven with gooey cheese and your favorite marinara sauce. This dish freezes well, so it's perfect to gift to new parents, along with a batch of Chocolate Rice Crunch Cookies (page 100).

Olive oil, for greasing the pan

12 ounces marinara sauce

1 (20-ounce) container fresh cheese ravioli

1 cup shredded mozzarella cheese

½ cup shredded Parmesan cheese

1 teaspoon freshly ground black pepper

½ teaspoon salt

¼ cup freshly chopped parsley

1. Preheat the oven to 400°F and grease a 9-by-13-inch baking dish with olive oil.

2. Spread 1 cup of marinara sauce over the bottom of the prepared baking dish. Arrange half of the ravioli over the sauce. Top with ½ cup of mozzarella and ¼ cup of Parmesan. Season with the pepper and salt. Layer on top the remaining ravioli, then the remaining ½ cup of sauce, ½ cup of mozzarella, and ¼ cup of Parmesan.

3. Cover the baking dish with aluminum foil and bake for 20 minutes. Remove the foil and continue baking for about 5 minutes more to brown the cheese. Top it with the parsley to serve.

MAKE-AHEAD TIP: This dish is a great make-ahead meal. To freeze, assemble the dish through step 2 in a freezer-safe baking dish or aluminum pan. Top it with foil and a lid, if possible, and store it in the freezer for up to one month. Thaw the ravioli for one hour before baking. Bake, covered, at 400°F, for about 40 minutes, or until heated through.

CREAMY BUTTERNUT SQUASH RIGATONI

FREEZER-FRIENDLY, NUT-FREE

Serves 4   **Prep time:** 20 minutes   **Cook time:** 55 minutes

There's nothing more soul-soothing than a big bowl of flavorful, luscious, and slightly sweet pasta. This dish gets its creaminess mostly from butternut squash, so it's easy to make it vegan if that's what you prefer. Just substitute the whole milk for canned full-fat coconut milk and either omit the Parmesan cheese or use your favorite vegan Parmesan in its place.

1 butternut squash, peeled, seeded, and cut into 1-inch cubes

4 tablespoons olive oil, divided, plus more for drizzling

2 garlic cloves, peeled and smashed

1½ teaspoons kosher salt, plus more if needed

¾ teaspoon freshly ground black pepper, plus more if needed

1 cup water

¾ cup whole milk

1 pound dry rigatoni

1 cup grated Parmesan cheese, plus more for serving

1. Preheat the oven to 400°F. Line a baking sheet with parchment paper or a silicone baking mat.

2. In a large bowl, toss the butternut squash with 2 tablespoons of oil. Arrange the coated squash in an even layer on the prepared baking sheet, along with the smashed garlic. Cook for 25 to 30 minutes, or until the squash is tender. Let cool slightly.

3. Transfer the squash and garlic to a food processor and add the salt and pepper. Puree until smooth.

4. Heat the remaining 2 tablespoons of oil in a large skillet set over medium heat. Add the pureed squash, water, and milk. Simmer for about 10 minutes, or until the sauce thickens slightly. Taste and adjust the seasonings as needed.

5. Meanwhile, bring a large pot of water to a boil over high heat and boil the pasta according to package directions. Reserve 1 cup of the pasta water after the pasta is done. Drain the pasta and set aside.

6. Add the pasta to the sauce with a splash of the reserved pasta water, tossing to combine. Remove the pot from the heat and add the Parmesan, tossing to combine. Thin the pasta sauce with a little of the reserved pasta water, if needed. Serve with additional Parmesan and a drizzle of olive oil, if desired.

INGREDIENT TIP: If fresh butternut squash is out of season or hard to find, frozen butternut squash works perfectly for this. Simply steam two (10-ounce) bags in the microwave according to package directions. Since you're not roasting the squash, you can use just one garlic clove and add it to the blender raw with the steamed butternut squash. Bonus: You'll cut down on about 30 minutes of cooking time, as well!

SPAGHETTI AGLIO E OLIO WITH ZUCCHINI

DAIRY-FREE, NUT-FREE, UNDER 30 MINUTES, VEGAN

Serves 4   **Prep time:** 5 minutes   **Cook time:** 25 minutes

Spaghetti *aglio e olio* (olive oil and garlic) is the perfect example of why simplicity works when it comes to cooking. Since the pasta has an opportunity to shine here, I love going for a high-quality spaghetti noodle with a rustic cut to soak up all of the olive oil and garlic flavor. If you have a local Italian market, that would be a wonderful place to find a nice pasta.

1 (16-ounce) package spaghetti noodles

½ cup olive oil

6 garlic cloves, minced

¼ teaspoon crushed red pepper flakes

1 medium zucchini, diced

½ teaspoon salt

¼ teaspoon freshly ground black pepper

¼ cup freshly chopped parsley

1. Bring a large pot of water to a boil over high heat. Add the pasta and cook according to package directions. Reserve ½ cup of the pasta water after the pasta is done. Drain the pasta and set aside.

2. Heat the oil in a large skillet over medium heat. Add the garlic, red pepper flakes, zucchini, salt, and black pepper and sauté for 5 to 7 minutes, or until the garlic is lightly golden and the zucchini is tender.

3. Add the spaghetti to the garlic and olive oil mixture, along with the reserved pasta water. Toss the pasta until evenly coated in the sauce and finish with the parsley on top. Serve warm.

COOKING TIP: If you can swing it, I like to time this dish so the pasta and sauce are done right around the same time. Transferring steaming hot pasta to the sauce allows it to absorb all of the aromatic flavor, making for a more balanced and well-rounded dish.

CAULIFLOWER FETTUCCINE ALFREDO

FREEZER-FRIENDLY, NUT-FREE

Serves 4   **Prep time:** 10 minutes   **Cook time:** 30 minutes

I'm typically not a fan of recipes that masquerade as other recipes, as referenced in my Teriyaki Cauliflower (page 67). I will, however, make one exception for cauliflower Alfredo, because it's that good. If you turn your nose up at all of the cauliflower hype, hear me out. This sauce is so creamy, so flavorful, and it perfectly coats every noodle. Be prepared for the looks of awe when you finally reveal that it's made out of cauliflower.

1 (16-ounce) package fettuccine noodles

1 medium cauliflower head, cut into small florets

6 garlic cloves

1½ cups whole milk or plant-based milk

1½ cups grated Parmesan cheese

1½ teaspoons salt

1 teaspoon freshly ground black pepper

1. Bring a large pot of water to a boil over high heat. Add the pasta and cook according to package directions. Reserve ½ cup of the pasta water after the pasta is done. Drain the pasta and set aside.

2. Using the same pot, bring another large pot of water to a boil. Add the cauliflower, cover, and cook for 8 to 10 minutes, or until fork-tender. Add the garlic for the last 2 minutes.

3. Add the cooked cauliflower and garlic to a high-speed blender or food processor. Add the milk and carefully puree until smooth.

4. Transfer the cauliflower sauce to a large skillet over medium heat and cook, whisking, for about 5 minutes, until slightly thickened. Stir in the Parmesan, salt, and pepper. Continue stirring until the sauce coats the back of a spoon. If it looks a little too thick, thin it out with ¼ to ½ cup of the reserved pasta water. Add the cooked fettuccine to the skillet and toss to fully coat. Serve warm.

LENTIL GOULASH

DAIRY-FREE, FREEZER-FRIENDLY, NUT-FREE, UNDER 30 MINUTES, VEGAN
Serves 4   **Prep time:** 10 minutes   **Cook time:** 20 minutes

Chances are good that someone in your family has their own rendition of American goulash. A few constants in most goulash recipes are elbow noodles, tomatoes, paprika, and, traditionally, beef. This vegan adaptation uses lentils as the main protein source, and let me tell you, it would make anyone's grand-parents proud. I like serving mine with a big dollop of Greek yogurt or sour cream on top.

1 (8-ounce) package elbow noodles

2 (14-ounce) cans diced tomatoes with garlic, divided

2 tablespoons olive oil

1 yellow onion, diced

1 (15-ounce) can brown lentils

1½ teaspoons paprika

1 teaspoon salt

½ teaspoon freshly ground black pepper

1. Bring a large pot of water to a boil over high heat. Add the pasta and cook according to package directions. Drain the pasta and set aside.

2. In the pitcher of a blender, combine 1 can of diced tomatoes with garlic and puree on high for about 1 minute, until smooth. Set aside.

3. Heat the oil in a large pot or Dutch oven over medium-high heat. Add the onion and sauté for 4 to 5 minutes, until translucent. Add the pureed tomatoes and the remaining 1 can of diced tomatoes with garlic, along with the lentils, paprika, salt, and pepper. Bring the mixture to a simmer, then reduce the heat to medium-low. Simmer for 5 minutes, then add the cooked pasta. Stir well to combine. Serve warm.

VARIATION TIP: Traditional goulash is pretty spice- and herb-heavy. If you have a fully stocked spice cabinet, you can add 1 teaspoon each of garlic powder, onion powder, dried oregano, dried basil, and dried parsley, and even a pinch of red pepper flakes if you like things spicy.

CORN AND RICOTTA BAKED ZITI

FREEZER-FRIENDLY, NUT-FREE

Serves 4 **Prep time:** 5 minutes **Cook time:** 40 minutes

If ever there was a baked pasta meant for warmer weather, this is the one. The sweet corn and ricotta combination is oddly refreshing and comforting at the same time. I picture this dish served at a late summer potluck alongside a Tomato Galette (page 76) and a big jug of lemonade. Top this ziti with fresh basil or serve it with a dollop of Simple Pesto (page 106) for an herbaceous bite.

1 (16-ounce) package ziti noodles

1 teaspoon olive oil

16 ounces whole-milk ricotta cheese

2 cups whole milk

3 garlic cloves, chopped

1½ teaspoons salt

¼ teaspoon freshly ground black pepper

2 cups frozen corn kernels

1. Bring a large pot of water to a boil over high heat. Add the pasta and cook according to package directions. Drain the pasta and set aside.

2. Meanwhile, preheat the oven to 425°F. Coat a 9-by-13-inch baking dish with the oil and set aside.

3. In a large bowl, whisk together the ricotta cheese, milk, garlic, salt, and pepper until smooth. Add the cooked pasta and corn, and stir everything together until well combined. Transfer the mixture to the prepared baking dish. Cover the dish with aluminum foil and bake for about 30 minutes, until bubbling. Serve warm.

GNOCCHI A LA VODKA

FREEZER-FRIENDLY, NUT-FREE, UNDER 30 MINUTES

Serves 4   **Prep time:** 5 minutes   **Cook time:** 15 minutes

Part potato and part dumpling, gnocchi is an honorary sibling in the pasta family. Their fluffy, porous texture easily absorbs the sauce and is a foolproof starch to add to any meal. They only take two to three minutes to cook, so they're basically on the table as quick as whatever sauce you pair them with. This simple vodka sauce comes together in about five minutes, so you can have the whole meal on the table in a flash.

1 (16-ounce) package fresh gnocchi

2 tablespoons olive oil

2 garlic cloves, minced

½ cup vodka

½ cup tomato paste

1½ cups heavy (whipping) cream

1 teaspoon salt

½ teaspoon freshly ground black pepper

1. Bring a large pot of water to a boil over high heat. Add the gnocchi and cook according to package directions. Drain the gnocchi and set aside.

2. Heat the oil in a large skillet over medium heat. Add the garlic and cook for about 30 seconds, until fragrant. Add the vodka and let it bubble for 30 seconds. Remove the skillet from the heat and whisk in the tomato paste until smooth. Return the pan to the heat, stir in the cream, and reduce the heat to medium-low. Cook for 2 to 3 minutes, until thickened. Season with the salt and pepper. Add the cooked gnocchi and stir to fully coat. Serve warm.

INGREDIENT TIP: You can substitute the vodka for the juice of one lemon and three-quarters of a cup of water or vegetable broth.

SAUCY SOBA NOODLES

DAIRY-FREE, FREEZER-FRIENDLY, UNDER 30 MINUTES, VEGAN
Serves 4   **Prep time:** 5 minutes   **Cook time:** 15 minutes

Every year for my birthday, I want either sushi, ramen, or some form of saucy soba noodle. I'm a creature of habit, what can I say? I chose soba noodles for this dish because they have a nutty, earthy taste that can stand up to the bold flavors of soy and sesame. If you like spice, don't be shy with the Sriracha, or garnish your noodles with a squeeze of lime or sesame seeds if that's more your speed.

1 (10-ounce) package soba noodles

1 tablespoon toasted sesame oil

5 large scallions, white and green parts, thinly sliced at an angle

3 tablespoons soy sauce

1 tablespoon peanut butter

½ cup water

1. Bring a large pot of water to a boil over high heat. Add the noodles and cook according to package directions. Drain the noodles and run them under cold water to remove the starch and make the noodles less sticky. Set aside.

2. Heat the oil in a large skillet over medium heat. Add the scallions and sauté for about 1 minute, until fragrant. Add the soy sauce, peanut butter, and water to the pan and whisk until creamy. Bring to a gentle simmer and cook for 1 to 2 minutes, until it thickens. Turn off the heat and add the noodles, tossing them in the sauce until fully coated. Serve warm.

INGREDIENT TIP: Soba noodles are typically made from a combination of buckwheat and whole-wheat flour. While some brands are gluten-free, you should double-check the packaging if that's a requirement for you.

CREAMY COCONUT VERMICELLI

DAIRY-FREE, NUT-FREE, UNDER 30 MINUTES, VEGAN

Serves 4   **Prep time:** 10 minutes   **Cook time:** 10 minutes

I hope you're prepared for all the flavor we're getting ready to pack into 5 ingredients. Coconut, lime, and mint hit all the right notes and will set your taste buds aglow with excitement. Tender vermicelli noodles are the best vehicle to deliver the slurpy goodness, and crunchy carrots add texture, color, and, of course, loads of beta-carotene to the dish. I've never been more convinced of the power of vegetables than I am right now with this recipe.

6 tablespoons unsweetened coconut milk

3 tablespoons freshly squeezed lime juice (from about 2 small limes)

1 teaspoon salt

¼ cup olive oil

1 (8-ounce) package vermicelli noodles

½ cup shredded carrot

½ cup freshly chopped mint leaves

1. In a small bowl, combine the coconut milk, lime juice, and salt. Gradually stream in the oil, whisking constantly, until combined. Set aside.

2. Bring a large pot of water to a boil over high heat. Add the pasta and cook according to package directions. Drain the pasta and run it under cold water.

3. In a large bowl, toss the pasta with the sauce and carrots. Top it with the mint. Serve chilled.

PASTA PUTTANESCA

DAIRY-FREE, FREEZER-FRIENDLY, NUT-FREE, UNDER 30 MINUTES, VEGAN

Serves 4   **Prep time:** 5 minutes   **Cook time:** 25 minutes

As far as Italian pastas go, spaghetti *alla puttanesca* is a fairly recent invention originating in Naples. Since it's made out of pantry staples like spaghetti, tomatoes, olives, and capers, this bright and salty dish is easy to throw together when it seems like there's nothing else in the house to cook. I highly recommend serving this dish with a buttery slice of focaccia bread for sopping up every last bit of sauce.

1 (16-ounce) package spaghetti noodles

¼ cup olive oil

3 garlic cloves, minced

1 (28-ounce) can whole tomatoes, drained and roughly chopped

½ teaspoon salt

½ teaspoon freshly ground black pepper

½ cup pitted and halved kalamata olives

¼ cup capers

1. Bring a large pot of water to a boil over high heat. Add the pasta and cook according to package directions. Drain the pasta and set aside.

2. Heat the oil in a large skillet over medium heat. Add the garlic and sauté for about 1 minute, until fragrant. Add the tomatoes and season with the salt and pepper. Bring to a simmer. Cook the tomatoes for 8 to 10 minutes, stirring occasionally and breaking the tomatoes apart, until the tomatoes have broken down. Stir in the olives and capers. Add the cooked pasta to the sauce, tossing to coat. Serve warm.

AFTER-SCHOOL NOODLE O'S

FREEZER-FRIENDLY, NUT-FREE, ONE-POT

Serves 4 **Prep time:** 5 minutes **Cook time:** 30 minutes

If you grew up around the '80s and '90s like me, canned pasta, microwave TV dinners, and toaster oven pizzas were pretty much what we survived on. Thankfully, healthier options are much more mass-produced these days, and we even have homemade versions of our favorite childhood meals. Whether you have kids of your own now or you're still a big kid at heart, this nostalgic pasta will be a hit with your whole house.

¼ cup olive oil

4 garlic cloves, minced

1 (6-ounce) can tomato paste

1 teaspoon onion powder

1 teaspoon salt

½ teaspoon freshly ground black pepper

8 cups water

1 (16-ounce) package anellini pasta

⅔ cup grated Parmesan cheese

1. Heat the oil in a large, deep skillet over medium heat. Add the garlic and sauté for about 1 minute, until fragrant. Add the tomato paste, onion powder, salt, and pepper. Whisk for 1 to 2 minutes, until the tomato paste is fragrant.

2. Whisk in the water and increase the heat to high. Bring the mixture to a boil, then reduce the heat to medium-low. Add the pasta, stir to combine, and simmer for 12 to 15 minutes, stirring frequently. When the pasta is tender and the sauce is thickened, stir in the Parmesan. Serve warm.

MAKE-AHEAD TIP: This dish freezes wonderfully for quick lunches or busy weeknight dinners. If you're planning on doing this, I would recommend cooking the pasta for only seven or eight minutes so it doesn't get overcooked. You can take some of the dish out to freeze and continue cooking the rest if you like. Freeze in individual portions for up to four months.

SOUTHWEST-STYLE ORZO

DAIRY-FREE, NUT-FREE, UNDER 30 MINUTES, VEGAN

Serves 4   **Prep time:** 10 minutes   **Cook time:** 15 minutes

If you ask me, orzo is the unsung hero of the pasta world. They shine in cold pasta salads, do the heavy lifting as a simple side, and pack a punch as a main dish. You can serve this Southwest-style orzo hot or cold, and I love it both ways. You may eat it warm on the first day, and then happily eat the leftovers cold.

1 (16-ounce) package orzo

1 (15.5-ounce) can black beans, drained and rinsed

2 cups cherry tomatoes, halved

2 cups frozen corn, defrosted

¼ cup olive oil

Juice and zest of 1 lime

1 teaspoon salt

1 teaspoon freshly ground black pepper

1. Bring a large pot of water to a boil over high heat. Add the pasta and cook according to package directions. Drain the pasta and set aside.

2. Transfer the orzo to a large bowl. Add the black beans, tomatoes, and corn.

3. In a small bowl, whisk together the olive oil, lime juice and zest, salt, and pepper until combined. Pour the vinaigrette over the pasta mixture and gently toss to combine. Serve chilled or warm.

CUCUMBER DILL COUSCOUS SALAD

DAIRY-FREE, NUT-FREE, VEGAN

Serves 4   **Prep time:** 10 minutes, plus 5 to 7 minutes to cool
Cook time: 20 minutes

Does everyone have a favorite herb, or is it just me? Dill is by far my most used herb. Its grassy flavor with notes of anise is such a standout, making it ideal for 5-ingredient cooking. In this recipe, we're pairing it with briny olives, fresh cucumber, and zesty lemon for a Mediterranean-inspired pasta salad that works wonderfully for lunch prep for the week.

1 (16-ounce) package Israeli (pearl) couscous

¼ cup olive oil

Juice and zest of 1 lemon

1 teaspoon salt

½ teaspoon freshly ground black pepper

1 medium English cucumber, diced

⅔ cup pitted kalamata olives, halved or quartered

¼ cup freshly chopped dill fronds

1. Bring a large pot of water to a boil over high heat. Add the couscous and cook according to package directions. Drain the couscous and set aside for 5 to 7 minutes, until cooled.

2. In a large bowl, whisk together the olive oil, lemon juice and zest, salt, and pepper until combined.

3. Add the cooled couscous to the dressing, along with the cucumber, olives, and dill. Serve chilled or at room temperature.

INGREDIENT TIP: Israeli couscous (technically a pasta) is much larger than regular couscous, and it has a heartier, chewier texture more akin to traditional pasta. Israeli couscous is available at most grocery stores, but if you can't find it, I'd recommend subbing a short-cut pasta like orzo or elbows.

PESTO PASTA SALAD

UNDER 30 MINUTES

Serves 4   **Prep time:** 5 minutes, plus 5 to 7 minutes to cool
Cook time: 15 minutes

Pesto pasta salad is the consummate chilled pasta dish. Whether you're making this for a friend, a soiree, or a work meeting, this recipe is fail-safe. You can't go wrong with a fun noodle, juicy tomatoes, creamy mozzarella, and homemade pesto. However, if you want to add a bit more nutrition and a peppery flavor, stir in a couple handfuls of arugula right before serving.

1 pound fusilli noodles

1 cup cherry tomatoes, halved

8 ounces fresh mozzarella, cut into bite-size pieces

½ cup finely chopped red onion

¼ teaspoon salt

⅛ teaspoon freshly ground black pepper

1 cup Simple Pesto (page 106), or store-bought

1. Bring a large pot of water to a boil over high heat. Add the pasta and cook according to package directions. Drain the pasta and set aside for 5 to 7 minutes, until cooled.

2. In a large bowl, combine the cooled pasta, cherry tomatoes, mozzarella, red onion, salt, pepper, and pesto. Toss until fully combined. Serve chilled. The salad will keep in an airtight container in the refrigerator for 3 to 5 days.

   MAKE-AHEAD TIP: This pasta salad is even better the next day! The salad may absorb some of the dressing as it sits, so if it seems a little dry when you serve it, just add a drizzle of olive oil to loosen it up.

LAVA CAKE, PAGE 102

CHAPTER SEVEN

Desserts and Staples

RASPBERRY CHIA MOUSSE

DAIRY-FREE, FREEZER-FRIENDLY, GLUTEN-FREE, ONE-POT, VEGAN

Serves 4   **Prep time:** 10 minutes, plus 4 hours to chill

If you're someone who has to have a little nibble of something sweet after every meal, welcome. This cookbook is a safe space for you. This dessert is similar to the Coconut Chocolate Chia Pudding (page 16) you may know and love, but blended to make an ultra-creamy mousse-like treat. Not a fan of raspberries? No problem. Any fruit will do. You can even add a quarter cup of cocoa powder for a nice chocolatey flavor.

2 cups almond milk

1 cup fresh or frozen raspberries

2 tablespoons maple syrup

½ teaspoon vanilla extract

Pinch salt

½ cup chia seeds

1. In a blender, combine the milk, raspberries, maple syrup, vanilla, and salt and blend until smooth.

2. Add the chia seeds and blend on high for about 1 minute, or until creamy.

3. Pour the mousse into 4 glass jars with lids, and refrigerate for at least 4 hours or overnight.

VARIATION TIP: This mousse is delicious as is for dessert, or you can add a ton of your favorite toppings to make it a fun and hearty breakfast or snack. I like adding Cinnamon Orange Granola (page 17), whole fruit, seeds, and a spoonful of nut butter.

YOGURT PANNA COTTA

GLUTEN-FREE, NUT-FREE

Serves 4   **Prep time:** 15 minutes, plus 6 hours to chill   **Cook time:** 15 minutes

When you invite friends over for an impromptu dinner but can't be bothered to bake, this panna cotta will be a lifesaver. They're as impressive as they are easy and will chill in the refrigerator while you make the rest of your meal. Top your plated panna cotta with some fresh fruit and a drizzle of chocolate sauce or honey for an elegant touch.

Nonstick cooking spray

1 cup heavy (whipping) cream, divided

1 vanilla bean, or 1 tablespoon vanilla extract

1½ teaspoons agar-agar

½ cup plain Greek yogurt

⅓ cup honey

1. Spray 4 (6-ounce) ramekins with nonstick cooking spray.

2. In a medium saucepan, pour in the cream. Split the vanilla bean in half lengthwise and with the back of your knife, scrape out the inside of the vanilla bean and add it to the pan with the agar-agar. Whisk the mixture and turn on the heat to medium. Allow it to bubble around the edges for 3 minutes. Continuously whisk the cream as it boils until everything is combined and no lumps remain. Turn off the heat, cover, and let sit for 5 minutes to allow the vanilla to steep.

3. In a medium bowl, whisk together the yogurt and honey until smooth. Pour the cream mixture into the yogurt mixture and whisk everything together until smooth and creamy.

4. Divide the mixture among the 4 prepared ramekins, cover, and place in the refrigerator for at least 6 hours to set. When ready to serve, unmold onto a dish and serve cold.

   SERVING TIP: Your panna cotta should come out of the ramekin fairly easily. If not, you can dunk the bottom of the ramekin in warm water to loosen it up first.

CHOCOLATE RICE CRUNCH COOKIES

DAIRY-FREE, FREEZER-FRIENDLY, UNDER 30 MINUTES, VEGAN

Makes 24 cookies   **Prep time:** 10 minutes, plus 15 minutes to chill
Cook time: 5 minutes

Every time I spent the night with my grandparents as a kid, I could guarantee that there would always be a box of Little Debbie Star Crunch Cookies on the counter. I guess I get my sweet tooth from my grandpa. This no-bake recipe is slightly more nutritious than the store-bought version, but I think he would still approve. If you're a Midwesterner, think of these as chocolatey scotcheroos in cookie form.

5 cups crisp or brown rice cereal

1½ cups semisweet chocolate chips

1 cup almond butter or any nut butter

½ cup maple syrup

¼ cup coconut oil

1. Line a large baking sheet with parchment paper and set it aside.

2. Pour the cereal into a large bowl and set it aside.

3. In a medium microwave-safe bowl, combine the chocolate chips, almond butter, maple syrup, and coconut oil. Microwave in 30-second intervals, stirring between each interval, until the chocolate is melted. Set aside to cool slightly.

4. Pour the chocolate mixture over the cereal and mix until fully coated. Using a large cookie scoop, drop rounds onto the prepared baking sheet about 2 inches apart. Press each round into a disk and refrigerate for 15 minutes, until firm. Serve chilled or at room temperature.

WHITE CHOCOLATE PEANUT BUTTER CUPS

FREEZER-FRIENDLY, GLUTEN-FREE, UNDER 30 MINUTES

Makes 12 peanut butter cups

Prep time: 10 minutes, plus 15 minutes to chill   **Cook time:** 5 minutes

Can you believe that you can ease that peanut butter cup craving in less than 30 minutes at home? That's less than the time it would take you to track one down at the store; plus, this one's made with better ingredients. These are perfect for keeping in the freezer for that midnight sweet tooth or whipping up for a last-minute holiday gift. If dark or milk chocolate is more your jam, feel free to swap.

½ cup peanut butter

1 tablespoon maple syrup

Pinch salt

2 cups white chocolate chips

1 tablespoon coconut oil

1. Line a standard muffin tin with cupcake liners.

2. In a small bowl, whisk together the peanut butter, maple syrup, and salt until creamy.

3. In microwave-safe bowl, combine the chocolate chips and coconut oil. Microwave in 30-second intervals, stirring between each interval, until the chocolate is melted.

4. Spoon a layer of the melted chocolate into the muffin liners. Add about a teaspoon of the peanut butter mixture on top. Add more melted chocolate into each liner to cover the peanut butter. Place the muffin tin in the freezer for 15 minutes to firm up the white chocolate. Serve chilled.

MAKE-AHEAD TIP: If stored in an airtight container, these peanut butter cups will keep for up to six months in the freezer. Just take one out when the craving strikes and let it sit at room temperature for about 10 minutes to soften, or enjoy frozen!

LAVA CAKE

NUT-FREE, UNDER 30 MINUTES

Makes 4 cakes   **Prep time:** 10 minutes   **Cook time:** 20 minutes

Nothing says date night quite like individual luscious lava cakes baked to perfection. That gooey chocolate center is pretty sexy, if you ask me. It will look like you're showing off your mad kitchen skills, but that's okay! Your date doesn't have to know just how easy these are. Serve the lava cakes with a big scoop of vanilla ice cream and some berries for good measure.

Nonstick
cooking spray

6 ounces semisweet
chocolate (not chips),
coarsely chopped

½ cup unsalted butter

½ cup
powdered sugar

¼ cup
all-purpose flour

⅛ teaspoon salt

2 large eggs plus
2 large egg yolks

1. Preheat the oven to 425°F. Spray 4 (6-ounce) ramekins with cooking spray. Set aside.

2. Place the chocolate and butter in a medium microwave-safe bowl. Microwave in 20-second intervals, stirring between each interval, until the chocolate is melted. Set aside to cool slightly.

3. In a small bowl, whisk together the powdered sugar, flour, and salt.

4. In another small bowl, whisk the eggs and egg yolks together until combined.

5. Pour the flour mixture and eggs into the bowl of melted chocolate. Stir everything together just until no lumps remain. Spoon the chocolate batter evenly into each prepared ramekin.

6. Place the ramekins onto a baking sheet for easy transfer. Bake for 12 to 14 minutes, until the edges appear firm but the tops are still soft. Allow to cool for 1 minute, then carefully cover each with a plate and turn over while they're still hot. Serve warm.

HONEY MUSTARD BARBECUE SAUCE

DAIRY-FREE, FREEZER-FRIENDLY, GLUTEN-FREE, NUT-FREE, ONE-POT, UNDER 30 MINUTES

Makes 1½ cups　　**Prep time:** 10 minutes

Listen, I don't want to get in the middle of anything, but Carolina gold barbecue sauce is at the top of the barbecue sauce pyramid. This pared-down variation may not be what's on the menu at most Southern joints, but it's perfect to throw together at home on a weeknight. Try it with the BBQ Tofu and Pineapple Sammies (page 53) or as a dipper for the Baked Pickle Chips (page 35).

½ cup yellow mustard

⅓ cup Dijon mustard

⅓ cup honey

¼ cup apple cider vinegar

1½ teaspoons freshly ground black pepper

3 teaspoons barbecue seasoning rub

In a medium bowl, whisk together the yellow mustard, Dijon, honey, vinegar, pepper, and barbecue rub. Chill until ready for use.

STORAGE TIP: This sauce will keep for up to two weeks in an airtight container in the refrigerator. You can also freeze small portions in an ice cube tray for up to three months.

GREEK YOGURT CUCUMBER RANCH

GLUTEN-FREE, NUT-FREE, ONE-POT

Makes 2 cups   **Prep time:** 10 minutes, plus 1 hour to chill

When tzatziki and ranch are combined, you better believe you're going to have a field day dipping all the crudités. This dip will be a staple in your refrigerator, whether the kiddos are sopping it up with their fries or you're spooning it on top of falafel. If you get an eleventh-hour party invitation, make this before you get ready and bring a bag of pita chips for scooping, and you'll have an easy, healthy snack in a flash.

2 cups plain
Greek yogurt

1 English cucumber,
shredded and
squeezed of excess
moisture

1 garlic clove, minced

Juice and zest
of 1 lemon

1 (1-ounce) packet
ranch seasoning
(see tip)

1 tablespoon olive oil

½ teaspoon salt

¼ teaspoon freshly
ground black pepper

In a medium bowl, stir together the Greek yogurt, cucumber, garlic, lemon juice and zest, ranch seasoning, oil, salt, and pepper. Cover and chill for 1 hour before serving. This will keep in an airtight container for up to 1 week.

VARIATION TIP: It's simple to swap the Greek yogurt for your favorite dairy-free yogurt to make this dip vegan, but watch out for milk powder in the ranch seasoning packet. You can find some dairy-free specialty ranch mix, but if those aren't accessible, just add one tablespoon of dried parsley, one tablespoon of dried chives, three-quarters teaspoon of granulated garlic, and a quarter teaspoon of paprika in place of the ranch seasoning.

BALSAMIC GLAZE

DAIRY-FREE, GLUTEN-FREE, NUT-FREE, ONE-POT, UNDER 30 MINUTES

Makes ½ cup   **Prep time:** 5 minutes   **Cook time:** 15 minutes

I have mentioned balsamic glaze numerous times in this book, but that's because it's a food accessory that just adds the perfect something to every dish. From pasta and sandwiches to salads and appetizers, there's nothing that couldn't be made better with a drizzle of balsamic glaze. It's a staple in my kitchen. To add an extra pop of rich flavor to Lemon Hummus (page 32), swirl in a spoonful before serving.

1 cup balsamic
vinegar

2 tablespoons honey

1. In a small saucepan over medium heat, bring the vinegar to a simmer. Whisk in the honey and return to a simmer. Reduce the heat to medium-low.

2. Lightly simmer, stirring occasionally, for 7 to 10 minutes, until it is reduced by half and starts to thicken. Pour the glaze into a glass jar and cover with a lid to store.

   MAKE-AHEAD TIP: If stored in an airtight container, this balsamic glaze will keep for up to one month in the refrigerator. I like to store it in a condiment squeeze bottle with a cap so I can easily drizzle some whenever the urge strikes.

SIMPLE PESTO

FREEZER-FRIENDLY, GLUTEN-FREE, ONE-POT, UNDER 30 MINUTES
Makes 1¼ cups   **Prep time:** 10 minutes

This simple pesto is essential in the Pesto Pasta Salad (page 95), but don't stop there; it's downright delicious when added to so many other dishes in this book and beyond. I prefer it to tomato sauce on pizza, and I love to spread it on grilled cheese. On your next pasta night, fill a small dish with olive oil, a spoonful of Balsamic Glaze (page 105), and this pesto, and you'll have the most wonderful dip for your baguette.

⅓ cup pine nuts

2 large garlic cloves, roughly chopped

2 cups packed fresh basil

½ teaspoon salt

¼ teaspoon freshly ground black pepper

⅔ cup olive oil, plus more for drizzling

½ cup grated Parmesan cheese

1. In a food processor, combine the pine nuts and garlic. Process for about 20 seconds, until finely chopped. Add the basil, salt, and pepper and process for about 1 minute, until the mixture starts to stick together and becomes pasty. With the processor running, slowly pour in the olive oil and blend until everything is uniform. Add the Parmesan and process for 1 additional minute.

2. Transfer the pesto to a glass jar and drizzle with a thin layer of olive oil to store. It will keep in the refrigerator for 1 week.

   INGREDIENT TIP: This recipe is a great way to use up excess basil in the summer, as well as other greens like parsley or arugula. Freeze the pesto in small portions in an ice cube tray for up to six months.

GARLIC AIOLI

DAIRY-FREE, GLUTEN-FREE, NUT-FREE, ONE-POT, UNDER 30 MINUTES

Makes 1 cup   **Prep time:** 5 minutes

Why use plain mayonnaise on your sandwiches and in dips when you can add a few standard ingredients to take the flavor over the top? Traditional home-made aioli is a blended mixture of egg yolks, olive oil, Dijon mustard, garlic, and lemon juice; however, this version uses mayonnaise to make things incredibly easy. Whatever you choose to scoop this with or slather it on will disappear as quickly as it takes to make it.

1 cup mayonnaise

2 tablespoons freshly squeezed lemon juice

3 garlic cloves, finely minced

1 tablespoon finely chopped fresh parsley

½ teaspoon salt

½ teaspoon freshly ground black pepper

1. Whisk together the mayonnaise, lemon juice, garlic, parsley, salt, and pepper until well combined.

2. Store in an airtight jar in the refrigerator for up to 10 days.

INGREDIENT TIP: When I'm using raw garlic in a dish, I like to make sure it's chopped as fine as possible. To do this, you can use a zester to grate the garlic or run your knife through it at least 10 times. You can also use the flat side of your knife to push the chopped garlic back and forth on your cutting board until it's almost a paste. When it's done, you can also allow the aioli to sit in the refrigerator for an hour before serving to allow the garlic flavor to blend in and mellow out a bit.

Measurements and Conversions

VOLUME EQUIVALENTS (LIQUID)

US STANDARD	US STANDARD (OUNCES)	METRIC (APPROXIMATE)
2 tablespoons	1 fl. oz.	30 mL
¼ cup	2 fl. oz.	60 mL
½ cup	4 fl. oz.	120 mL
1 cup	8 fl. oz.	240 mL
1½ cups	12 fl. oz.	355 mL
2 cups or 1 pint	16 fl. oz.	475 mL
4 cups or 1 quart	32 fl. oz.	1 L
1 gallon	128 fl. oz.	4 L

OVEN TEMPERATURES

FAHRENHEIT (F)	CELSIUS (C) (APPROXIMATE)
250°F	120°C
300°F	150°C
325°F	165°C
350°F	180°C
375°F	190°C
400°F	200°C
425°F	220°C
450°F	230°C

VOLUME EQUIVALENTS (DRY)

US STANDARD	METRIC (APPROXIMATE)
⅛ teaspoon	0.5 mL
¼ teaspoon	1 mL
½ teaspoon	2 mL
¾ teaspoon	4 mL
1 teaspoon	5 mL
1 tablespoon	15 mL
¼ cup	59 mL
⅓ cup	79 mL
½ cup	118 mL
⅔ cup	156 mL
¾ cup	177 mL
1 cup	235 mL
2 cups or 1 pint	475 mL
3 cups	700 mL
4 cups or 1 quart	1 L

WEIGHT EQUIVALENTS

US STANDARD	METRIC (APPROXIMATE)
½ ounce	15 g
1 ounce	30 g
2 ounces	60 g
4 ounces	115 g
8 ounces	225 g
12 ounces	340 g
16 ounces or 1 pound	455 g

Index

Acknowledgments

It almost seems unfair that my name gets to be on the cover of this book when there are so many people who made it possible: To my husband, Matt, who defines selflessness with every sacrifice that he makes for me to succeed in my dreams.

Thank you to each of the team members at Callisto Media that worked on this book.

Collaborating with a team that so highly values diversity, inclusivity, and innovation in every way has been an absolute dream.

I can't skip over the loyal readers of my blog, *My Modern Cookery*. Whether you're frequently in contact on social media or you're a silent scroller, my gratitude knows no bounds.

To my daughter, Norah, I thank you most of all. I hope that through my hard work, you see that women can achieve anything they desire, and not even the sky is the limit.

About the Author

Paige Rhodes is the founder of the *My Modern Cookery* blog, a recipe developer, food stylist, content creator, mother, and author of the book *The Home Cook's Guide to Journaling*. After showing an interest in both cooking and writing, she attended culinary school at Sullivan University in Louisville, Kentucky, where she built on her lifelong passion for the culinary arts.

She has written for many online and print publications such as *Hearst*, *Food52*, *Country Sampler*, *The Voice-Tribune*, and *Today's Woman Now*. She's been featured in Buzzfeed articles, the *Draper James* blog, Brit + Co, and many more. Paige has created a large community of home cooks who join her daily in her love for wholesome food, family, and conversation. You can find her blog at MyModernCookery.com or @mymoderncookery on all social media channels.

CPSIA information can be obtained
at www.ICGtesting.com
Printed in the USA
JSHW011326230122
22195JS00003B/4